Look out for the
FREE HAT
Inside This Annual!

D1639367

SCISSORS ARE SHARP!
ASK AN ADULT FOR HELP!

CONTENTS

Pedigree

Published 2013.
Pedigree Books Limited, Beech Hill House, Walnut Gardens, Exeter, Devon EX4 4DH
www.pedigreebooks.com / books@pedigreegroup.co.uk

The Pedigree trademark, email and website addresses, are the sole and exclusive
properties of Pedigree Group Limited, used under licence in this publication.

IT'S ALL ABOUT ASH

It seems a long time since Ash started out as a young Trainer in Pallet Town, but his passion and resolve are stronger than ever! Ash is determined to succeed in the Unova League tournament, even when the odds are stacked against him. Ash knows he can be impulsive, rash and hasty at times, but he's learned a lot during his travels. Now that he's visited many regions and earned an enviable collection of Gym Badges, he's ready to show the world what he can do!

GET TO KNOW... ASH MINI QUIZ

1. WHAT DOES ASH ASPIRE TO BE?
A. a Pokémon Breeder
B. a Pokémon Master
C. a Pokémon Connoisseur

2. WHAT IS ASH'S SURNAME?
A. Kendo
B. Ketchum
C. Kirsten

3. WHAT POKÉMON TYPE IS ASH'S SCRAGGY?
A. Dark-Fighting
B. Dark-Flying
C. Dark-Poison

As the Unova League rages on, Ash will count on his friends for support and encouragement. Pikachu is Ash's best friend and is the Pokémon that has been there since the early days in Kanto. The sparky Electric-type rides on Ash's shoulder, always ready to protect Ash if danger arises. During his time in Unova, Ash has also collected a loyal crew of Pokémon. From Snivy to Scraggy, every one has what it takes to pull out all the stops in the battle arena.

HERE'S LOOKING AT YOU
PIKACHU

Pikachu has been Ash's Pokémon from the very begining, but he certainly wasn't the Trainer's first choice. On the day he was due to report in to Professor Oak, Ash slept through his alarm. He'd hoped to be teamed up with a Squirtle, but by the time he arrived at the lab Pikachu was the only Pokémon available. Sparks flew! At first the two feisty personalities didn't get along, but over time Ash and Pikachu have become firm friends.

Whenever Ash finds himself in trouble, Pikachu comes out fighting, even when the odds are stacked against him. For his part, Ash always returns the favour. Being a very rare and covetable Pokémon, Pikachu has been kidnapped many times. Ash would go anywhere and do anything to protect his friend – nobody can drive a wedge between these two! Pikachu is the only one of Ash's Pokémon not to travel in a Poké Ball. Pikachu wouldn't have it any other way.

GET TO KNOW....
PIKACHU
MINI QUIZ

1. WHAT DOES PIKACHU STORE IN ITS CHEEKS?

A. Electricity ☐

B. Poffins ☐

C. Berries ☐

2. WHICH ONE OF THESE IS NOT A PIKACHU BATTLE MOVE?

A. Thunderbolt ☐

B. Iron Tail ☐

C. Headbutt ☐

3. HOW DOES PIKACHU GET AROUND?

A. He rides in an electric car ☐

B. He travels in a Poké Ball ☐

C. He sits on Ash's shoulder ☐

INSTANTLY IRIS

Iris was Ash's first new friend in the Unova region and now she roams everywhere with him. The raven-haired youngster comes from a small village that specialises in raising Dragon-type Pokémon. Ever since she can remember, Iris has had one dream — to become a fully-fledged Dragon Master. She still has lots to learn, but nothing can rival her commitment and dedication. The way Iris sees it, every day is a brand new opportunity for something awesome to happen!

Iris isn't alone in her travels. Aside from Ash and Cilan, she is devoted to a plucky little Axew. The Dragon-type is still cutting its teeth at battling, but it's got all the signs of a champ! Axew and Iris are learning together every step of the way, collecting Pokémon as they go.

Now that she's exploring the world outside her village, Iris is enthralled by the variety Unova has to offer. Breathtaking battles, exotic Pokémon and brand new friends wait around every corner. Ash's journey to the Vertress City Gym is the climax of that adventure — one she's been waiting for all her life!

GET TO KNOW... IRIS MINI QUIZ

WHICH OF THESE POKÉMON HAS IRIS ALSO CAPTURED?
A. Stunfisk ☐
B. Emolga ☐
C. Leavanny ☐

WHAT IS AXEW'S NEXT EVOLUTION?
A. Haxorus ☐
B. Fraxure ☐
C. Hydreigon ☐

WHICH WORDS DESCRIBE IRIS BEST?
A. Confident and wild ☐
B. Shy and quiet ☐
C. Thoughtful and bookish ☐

FUN WITH CILAN

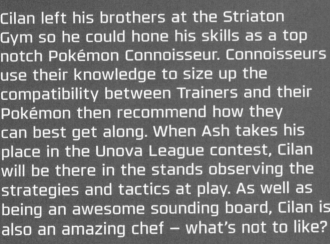

Ash has lost count of the times he's thanked his lucky stars for hooking him up with Cilan! Cilan may only be a new friend, but his sense and wisdom have bailed Ash out of trouble time and time again. As one of the three Striaton Gym Leaders, Cilan has bags of Unova experience. He's the person Trainers turn to when they need some smart and snappy Pokémon advice.

Cilan left his brothers at the Striaton Gym so he could hone his skills as a top notch Pokémon Connoisseur. Connoisseurs use their knowledge to size up the compatibility between Trainers and their Pokémon then recommend how they can best get along. When Ash takes his place in the Unova League contest, Cilan will be there in the stands observing the strategies and tactics at play. As well as being an awesome sounding board, Cilan is also an amazing chef – what's not to like?

GET TO KNOW... CILAN MINI QUIZ

WHICH POKÉMON DOES CILAN TRAVEL WITH?
A. Panpour
B. Patrat
C. Pansage

WHAT STANDS OUT ABOUT THE WAY CILAN SPEAKS?
A. He's always cracking jokes
B. He's very grumpy
C. Everything sounds like a recipe

WHAT ARE THE NAMES OF CILAN'S BROTHERS?
A. Tristan and Tim
B. Chili and Cress
C. Steve and Samuel

BRING ON BIANCA

Ash is always wary when he runs into Bianca — the accident-prone Trainer has a habit of soaking him with water! Bianca doesn't travel around with Ash, Iris and Cilan, but they often cross paths. Since setting out from her home in Nuvema Town, Bianca has popped up in all sorts of locations!

Bianca has a good heart, but she can be easily distracted. Despite working hard to capture her own crew of Pokémon, the young Trainer has landed herself in some pretty sticky situations. When she battled and lost out to Elesa at the Nimbasa City Gym, her father nearly forced her to come home, worried that she was too inexperienced to be on the road. Luckily Ash stepped in to convince him that Bianca could make it on her own in Unova.

Now that the finals of the Unova League are taking place, Bianca has come to Vertress City. Aside from catching up with friends and eating Casteliacones, she can't wait to try her luck against her rivals.

GET TO KNOW... BIANCA MINI QUIZ

1. WHICH OF THESE POKÉMON HAVE BELONGED TO BIANCA?
A. Minccino ☐
B. Foongus ☐
C. Ducklett ☐

2. WHAT IS BIANCA'S WEAKNESS IN THE BATTLE GYM?
A. Choosing poor moves ☐
B. Keeps changing her mind ☐
C. Soft spot for cute Pokémon ☐

3. WHAT WAS BIANCA'S FIRST POKÉMON?
A. Snivy ☐
B. Tepig ☐
C. Oshawott ☐

THE TIP FROM TRIP

Ash and Trip have been arch-rivals from the get-go! Both Trainers are strong-willed, focussed and super competitive. Trip hasn't been a Trainer for as long as Ash, but there is no limit to his ambition. He will, quite simply, do anything he has to do to become the best of the best. Sometimes Trip lets his resolve get in the way of friendship, but he's gradually starting to realise that even top Trainers need to show some heart every now and then.

Trip first got inspired when he watched Alder, the charismatic Unova League Champion do battle. Although he was still only a child, he never forgot Alder's sage advice to work hard and grow strong. Trip is a reserved character who usually guards his feelings, but he'd do anything to impress his hero!

When he's not challenging other Trainers, Trip prefers to travel alone. He likes to keep his rivals at a distance, whiling away the hours doing drills with his Pokémon instead. Ash respects him as a fighting force, but wishes he would lighten up every now and then. After all, the pair have more than a little in common! Both Ash and Trip have their sights set on the Unova League. Only time will tell who will come out on top...

GET TO KNOW.... TRIP mini quiz

1. WHO HAS WON THE MOST BATTLES – ASH OR TRIP?
A. Ash
B. Trip
C. It's a draw

2. WHICH OF THESE POKÉMON DOESN'T TRAVEL WITH TRIP?
A. Serperior
B. Frillish
C. Excavalier

3. WHO IS TRIP'S ROLE MODEL?
A. Alder
B. Caitlin
C. Stephan

REPORT TO OFFICER JENNY!

When there's trouble in Unova, there's only one person to call – Officer Jenny! She's brave and unswerving, with a sense of duty that runs to the core. Even when she's out-manoeuvred by the bad guys, Officer Jenny always looks the part. She wears a smart tan uniform and a hat with a special symbol on the front.

GET TO KNOW... OFFICER JENNY MINI QUIZ

1. WHICH POKÉMON OFTEN ACCOMPANIES OFFICER JENNY?
A. Herdier
B. Bouffalant
C. Riolu

2. WHAT MODE OF TRANSPORT DOES OFFICER JENNY USE?
A. Helicopter
B. Speedboat
C. Motor bike

NOW FOR NURSE JOY

Nurse Joy is always on hand to dispense her own special brand of treatment. Nurse Joy is kind, gentle and thoughtful, knowing just how to heal the sick and injured patients in her care. Whenever Ash's Pokémon need rest or medicine, he is sure to check into his nearest Pokémon Center. With Nurse Joy in charge, nobody remains poor for long!

GET TO KNOW... NURSE JOY MINI QUIZ

1. WHERE WOULD YOU FIND USUALLY NURSE JOY?
A. at the City Gym
B. in the market place
C. at the Pokémon Center

2. WHAT POKÉMON OFTEN WORKS ALONGSIDE THE NURSE IN UNOVA?
A. Braviary
B. Audino
C. Munna

SWOT UP ON PROFESSOR JUNIPER!

Professor Juniper runs the laboratory in the Unova region. She's a smart cookie who knows Pokémon inside and out! Whenever Ash is contemplating entering a battle he touches base with the Prof via video link. Professor Juniper sets new Trainers to the region on the right track, supplying them with their starter Pokémon.

GET TO KNOW... PROF JUNIPER mini quiz

1. HOW DOES PROFESSOR JUNIPER SPEND HER DAYS?
A. Studying Trainer stats ☐
B. Testing new medicines ☐
C. Researching Pokémon ☐

2. WHERE IS SHE RESIDENT PROFESSOR?
A. Striaton City ☐
B. Nuvema Town ☐
C. Pinwheel Forest ☐

GO TEAM ROCKET

Some people just don't seem to get the message! Despite Ash's constant attempts to throw them off, Team Rocket are still trying to track our hero down. Jessie, James and Meowth work for a criminal organisation that steals valuable Pokémon. The dastardly crew have their eyes on one prize – Ash's Pikachu! Luckily Ash and his friends are always on their guard.

GET TO KNOW... TEAM ROCKET mini quiz

1. WHAT IS SPECIAL ABOUT TEAM ROCKET'S MEOWTH?
A. Its claws are extra sharp ☐
B. It can talk like a human ☐
C. It has over nine lives ☐

2. WHAT IS THE NAME OF THE OUTFIT'S MYSTERIOUS BOSS?
A. Giovanni ☐
B. Giuseppe ☐
C. Luigi ☐

UNOVA POKÉDEX

Prepare for Pokédex paradise – this annual contains a vast list of species from the Unova region! Now you can have all the facts and stats you need at your fingertips, just like Ash! This fascinating resource is just the thing for debut Trainers right through to highly skilled Trainers looking to brush up on their knowledge and expertise.

BUG
Awesome Accelgor, electrically-charged Galvantula, septic Scolipede on pages 16-17

FLYING
The stormy power of Tornadus on pages 30-31

DARK
Stealthy Liepard, blade-wielding Pawniard, spitting Scrafty on pages 16-17

GHOST
Golden Cofagrigus, life sapping Litwick on pages 36 and 37

FIRE
Darmanitan's Fire Punch, blazing Simisear, smoke-snorting Tepig, on pages 30-31

ELECTRIC
Ravenous Eelektrik, tree-dwelling Emolga, short-fused Zebstrika, on pages 30-31

DRAGON
Druddigon the sun-seeker, thunderous Zekrom, on pages 30-31

FIGHTING
Conkeldurr's concrete pillars, elegant Mienfoo, muscle-bound Sawk, on pages 30-31

GRASS

Dancing Amoonguss, the glare of Serperior, fluffy Whimsicott on pages 36-37

GROUND

Excadrill the tunneller, the bite of Krookodile, thick-skinned Stunfisk on pages 36-37

ROCK

Swooping Archeops, mighty Gigalith, charging Terrakion on pages 72-73

NORMAL

Bouffalant's headbutt, Deerling's changeable fur, peace-loving Tranquill on pages 52-53

PSYCHIC

The mind powers of Gothitelle, floating Solosis, the winning ways of Victini on pages 52-53

WATER

Scalchop-slicing Dewott, the tremors of Palpitoad, flocking Swanna on pages 72-73

POISON

Rubbish-sucking Garbodor on pages 52-53

STEEL

Calm, collected Cobalion, gear-twisting Klingklang on pages 72-73

ICE

Beartic's freezing breath, blizzard-whipping Vanilluxe on pages 72-73

To make things easy, each Pokémon has been listed by type in alphabetical order and dual type Pokémon are listed under its first type. There are 17 categories to flick through, packed with an eye-boggling range of Unova species. Why not look up some of these highlights? You're bound to be knocked out by the jaw-dropping spectrum of behaviour and characteristics.

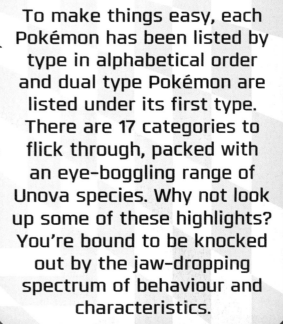

15

ACCELGOR

TYPE: Bug
CATEGORY: Shell Out
HEIGHT: 0.8m   WEIGHT: 25.3kg

Having shed its shell Accelgor is very light, moving like a ninja when it fights. It wraps itself in many layers of membrane to prevent dehydration.

CRUSTLE

TYPE: Bug-Rock
CATEGORY: Stone Home
HEIGHT: 1.4m   WEIGHT: 200.0kg

With its enormously powerful legs, Crustle can walk for days across arid land while carrying a heavy slab. Its battles for territory are vicious.

DURANT

TYPE: Bug-Steel
CATEGORY: Iron Ant
HEIGHT: 0.3m   WEIGHT: 33.0kg

Durant digs nests in the mountains to create mazes of linked tunnels. Covered in steel armour to protect from Heatmor, it attacks in a group.

DWEBBLE

TYPE: Bug-Rock
CATEGORY: Rock Inn
HEIGHT: 0.3m   WEIGHT: 14.5kg

The liquid from Dwebble's mouth melts through rock. It makes its home in a suitable rock, but if the rock is broken, it must find a replacement.

ESCAVALIER

TYPE: Bug-Steel
CATEGORY: Cavalry
HEIGHT: 1.0m   WEIGHT: 33.0kg

Escavalier wears a Shelmet's shell, and steel armour protects its body. It battles courageously even in trouble, attacking with its pointed spears.

GALVANTULA

TYPE: Bug-Electric
CATEGORY: EleSpider
HEIGHT: 0.8m   WEIGHT: 14.3kg

It traps prey with its electrically-charged web. If attacked, Galvantula can also spit out charged threads to create an electric barrier.

JOLTIK

TYPE: Bug-Electric
CATEGORY: Attaching
HEIGHT: 0.1m   WEIGHT: 0.6kg

Joltik clings to large Pokémon and absorbs static electricity, which it stores in an electric pouch. Joltik can drain electricity from outlets in houses.

KARRABLAST

TYPE: Bug
CATEGORY: Clamping
HEIGHT: 0.5m   WEIGHT: 5.9kg

This mysterious Pokémon targets Shelmet and evolves when it receives electrical stimulation while a Shelmet is present. Spits acid if threatened.

LARVESTA

TYPE: Bug-Fire
CATEGORY: Torch
HEIGHT: 1.1m   WEIGHT: 28.8kg

Larvesta dwells at the base of volcanoes. When it evolves, its entire body is wreathed in flames. Its five horns shoot fire.

LEAVANNY

TYPE: Bug-Grass
CATEGORY: Nurturing
HEIGHT: 1.2m   WEIGHT: 20.5kg

Using silk and the cutters on its arms, Leavanny weaves clothing for any small Pokémon it meets. It uses leaves to keep its eggs warm.

SCOLIPEDE

TYPE: Bug-Poison
CATEGORY: Megapede
HEIGHT: 2.5m   WEIGHT: 200.5kg

This aggressive Pokémon poisons targets by grabbing them with the claws around its neck. When it pursues a foe, it swiftly attacks with its horns.

SEWADDLE

TYPE: Bug-Grass
CATEGORY: Sewing
HEIGHT: 0.3m   WEIGHT: 2.5kg

To make clothes it chews up leaves and sews them together with thread from its mouth. Leavanny also make clothes to dress newly-hatched Sewaddle.

SHELMET

TYPE: Bug
CATEGORY: Snail
HEIGHT: 0.4m   WEIGHT: 7.7kg

Shelmet defends itself by shutting the lid of its shell and spitting poison. It evolves when both it and a Karrablast are bathed in electric-like energy.

SWADLOON

TYPE: Bug-Grass
CATEGORY: Leaf-Wrapped
HEIGHT: 0.5m   WEIGHT: 7.3kg

It wraps itself in leaves to keep away the cold. Swadloon forests have lush foliage, because the Swadloon turn fallen leaves into fertilising nutrients.

VENIPEDE

TYPE: Bug-Poison
CATEGORY: Centipede
HEIGHT: 0.4m   WEIGHT: 5.3kg

Venipede's poisonous bite can paralyse even the large avian Pokémon that hunt it. The feelers on its head and tail keep it aware of its surroundings.

VOLCARONA

TYPE: Bug-Fire
CATEGORY: Sun
HEIGHT: 1.6m   WEIGHT: 46.0kg

When Volcarona battles, its wings scatter ember scales, creating a sea of flames. Some say its fire replaced the sun when volcanic ash darkened the atmosphere.

WHIRLIPEDE

TYPE: Bug-Poison
CATEGORY: Curlipede
HEIGHT: 1.2m   WEIGHT: 58.5kg

Encased in a hard shell, Whirlipede rarely moves unless attacked. It can spin like a wheel and smash into its foes.

BISHARP

TYPE: Dark-Steel
CATEGORY: Sword Blade
HEIGHT: 1.6m   WEIGHT: 70.0kg

Bisharp hunts prey with a large group of Pawniard and battles to become their leader. It is expelled from the group if it loses.

DEINO

TYPE: Dark-Dragon
CATEGORY: Irate
HEIGHT: 0.8m   WEIGHT: 17.3kg

Approach Deino with care — unable to see, it bites and tackles to learn about its environment and has injuries all over its body. It is not a picky eater.

HYDREIGON

TYPE: Dark-Dragon
CATEGORY: Brutal
HEIGHT: 1.8m   WEIGHT: 160.0kg

This Pokémon registers anything that moves as a foe. Through all three of its heads can attack and devour, the heads on its arms have no brains.

LIEPARD

TYPE: Dark
CATEGORY: Cruel
HEIGHT: 1.1m   WEIGHT: 37.5kg

Many Trainers are attracted by the beautiful form and fur of this stealthy Pokémon. It appears and disappears without warning, striking by surprise.

MANDIBUZZ

TYPE: Dark-Flying
CATEGORY: Bone Vulture
HEIGHT: 1.2m   WEIGHT: 39.5kg

Mandibuzz uses bones to adorn itself and build its nest. It looks for weakened Pokémon, then swoops down to seize prey in its talons.

PAWNIARD

TYPE: Dark-Steel
CATEGORY: Sharp Blade
HEIGHT: 0.5m   WEIGHT: 10.2kg

Pawniard's body is made of blades. If its blades are dull from battling, it sharpens them on stones by the river. It fights under orders from Bisharp.

PURRLOIN

TYPE: Dark
CATEGORY: Devious
HEIGHT: 0.4m   WEIGHT: 10.1kg

Though Purrloin can attack with sharp claws, its cute act is a ruse to make targets drop their guard. Purrloin then steals the target's items.

SCRAFTY

TYPE: Dark-Fighting
CATEGORY: Hoodlum
HEIGHT: 1.1m   WEIGHT: 30.0kg

Scrafty spits acidic liquid and uses kicking attacks to smash concrete blocks. A group of Scrafty will attack anyone who enters their territory.

SCRAGGY

TYPE: Dark-Fighting
CATEGORY: Shedding
HEIGHT: 0.6m   WEIGHT: 11.8kg

Scraggy's skull is extremely thick, and it headbutts anyone who makes eye contact with it. It can shield itself by pulling its rubbery skin up to its neck.

VULLABY

TYPE: Dark-Flying
CATEGORY: Diapered
HEIGHT: 0.5m   WEIGHT: 9.0kg

Vullaby finds suitable bones and uses them to shield its rear, discarding them when it's ready to evolve. Unable to fly, it pursues weak Pokémon.

ZOROARK

TYPE: Dark
CATEGORY: Illusion Fox
HEIGHT: 1.6m   WEIGHT: 81.1kg

It can fool many people at the same time, hiding its lair with illusory scenery. Zoroark protect their pack by transforming into opponents.

ZORUA

TYPE: Dark
CATEGORY: Tricky Fox
HEIGHT: 0.7m   WEIGHT: 12.5kg

Zorua protects itself by concealing its true identity, transforming into people or other Pokémon. Supposedly, Zorua often resembles a silent child.

ZWEILOUS

TYPE: Dark-Dragon
CATEGORY: Hostile
HEIGHT: 1.4m   WEIGHT: 50.0kg

Zweilous always ends up overeating because its two heads compete for food. Once it has eaten all the food in its territory, it moves on.

MISSION: DEFEAT YOUR RIVAL!

Ash's adventures take a thrilling turn when he and his friends journey to Vertress City. The electrifying Unova League has begun with Ash unexpectedly pitted against Trip in the qualifying round! Can our hero emerge victorious?

The crowd roared. It seemed as if the whole of Vertress City had turned out to see Ash do battle with his rival! Ash's friends Cilan and Iris watched anxiously from the stands. The stakes were high – if Ash lost this he wouldn't be able to move on to the main event.

"Use Dragon Tail!" shouted Trip, sending his Serperior into the fray.

Pikachu tried to dodge the attack, but he was too slow. The lash of Serperior's tail sent him spinning to the side of the Battle Gym.

"No!" cried Ash.

Iris's face creased with worry. Pikachu had been hit hard!

"It's not just speed," sighed Cilan. "Serperior's attack power is a lot stronger, too."

Unova League presenter, Freddy the Scoop, looked down from the commentary box.

"Will Pikachu be able to continue?" he asked.

"Come on Pikachu," urged Ash. "Get up!"

The plucky Electric-type slowly rose to his feet, but Trip was quick to make the most of his advantage.

"How about this?" he asked. "OK Serperior. Energy Ball, go!"

A globe of white light pummelled Pikachu to the ground. Serperior batted its foe again and again, before coiling its tail around the Pokémon's neck. The expert Wrap move left Pikachu trapped and struggling to breathe.

Freddy the Scoop grinned. This match was hotting up!

"Poor Pikachu's caught!" cried Iris.

"If Serperior keeps squeezing with so much force," replied Cilan grimly," Pikachu is in real trouble."

Ash responded the only way he knew how – with Pikachu's signature Thunderbolt move! Iris trembled in her seat as Pikachu gave it everything he'd got.

Trip reacted quickly to the counterattack.

"Stick your tail into the ground!" he shouted, pointing to the dusty stadium floor.

Serperior followed its Trainer's order to the letter. The crowds gasped as the electric current from Pikachu ran straight down Serperior's tail, earthing itself in the ground below. Ash's attack hadn't done a thing!

"Serperior's using its tail like a ground wire to avoid any damage," announced Freddy the Scoop.

"All right, Serperior!" laughed Trip, "squeeze even harder!"

Ash watched helplessly as Serperior trapped Pikachu again. The Pokémon was locked tight!

Vital seconds were passing, but Ash was lost in thought. Trip had defeated him too many times already, he couldn't let it happen again! He desperately tried to find the strength he needed.

"If I lose now," he whispered, "my whole journey is a waste."

On the big screen, news of other contestants began to flash up. Ash's friend Bianca had got through, along with Virgil and Cameron. The victories were piling up at the Unova League Stadium!

"Ash and Trip are still battling… which one of them will claim victory?" recapped Freddy, "Pikachu's got big problems! I don't see any way Ash can win it!"

Iris and Cilan clenched their fists. Pikachu had to break free!

"Come on," shouted Cilan. "You can do this!"

As soon as their matches were over, Bianca, Stephan and Cameron rushed over to find out how their friend was getting on. They had all won their rounds – now it was Ash's turn! Cilan sadly explained that this battle wasn't going to plan.

"Pikachu can't seem to break free from Serperior's Wrap," he sighed. "The smell of victory is in the air for Trip."

Bianca gasped. Ash couldn't give up on his dreams already!

"Listen to me, Ash!" Cameron yelled. "If you want to become a Pokémon Master, don't lose the qualifying round right off the bat. I won my round and you've got to win yours, too!"

The Trainer and his Riolu swapped worried looks. There had to be some way for Pikachu to escape Serperior's clutches.

Trip smirked with confidence. He figured it was time to wrap this one up.

Ash was desperate. What was he going to do now?

"You can't give up now," he begged. "Pikachu Open your eyes!"

The Trainer hoped and waited... until the Pokémon finally returned his stare.

"That's it!" he yelled, spotting Pikachu's zigzag tail. "Use Iron Tail on the battlefield!"

Pikachu was only small, but there was no limit to his determination! Quick as a flash, the bold Electric-type transformed his tail into a glinting silver weapon, freeing himself from Serperior's vice grip.

"Way to go!" bellowed Ash.

Trip looked bewildered.

"What happened?" he muttered.

The crowd went wild to see Pikachu turn the tables.

"That was amazing!" squealed Iris.

Cilan agreed. If this was a taste of Ash's strategy, he couldn't wait to see some more!

"Serperior, go!"

"That's it!" grinned Ash, "Wind it up!"

At the very same instant, Pikachu and Serperior unleashed their full force on each other. The ground shook as the pair collided in an explosion of raw power.

Ka-boom!

Both Pokémon were sent tumbling to the ground.

"Pikachu?" whispered Ash, when the dust finally started to settle.

To the fans' surprise, the little Pokémon clambered back on his feet! His opponent, however, was not so lucky.

"Serperior is unable to battle," decided the judge. "Pikachu wins! And that means the match goes to Ash!"

"All right!" cheered the victorious Trainer. His Iron Tail and Electro Ball combination was a winner!

"Use Iron Tail again!" called Ash, keen to make the most of Pikachu's advantage.

Trip knew just how to respond. The crowd roared as the skillful Trainer sent Serperior straight back into the fray.

"Intercept it with Dragon Tail!"

Serperior's tail began to glow with intense energy. It lashed through the air, felling Pikachu's attack in a single, deft swipe. Pikachu groaned in surprise.

"Aha!" surmised Freddy the Scoop. "A clash between Iron Tail and Dragon Tail, and Dragon Tail wins!"

Trip's eyes flickered with excitement.

"You battled well," he smiled, "but it's over now…"

"Over?"

Ash glowered. Pikachu's cheeks crackled with electricity. The friends had to do something to take out that Dragon Tail!

Watching Pikachu get all charged up suddenly gave Ash had an awesome idea.

"Use a combination move with Iron Tail and Electro Ball!" he cried.

Pikachu didn't hesitate. His tail began to glint like metal. A sparking globe of electricity spun around it, growing more intense with every moment.

"You two are wasting your time," scoffed Trip.

After the match, Ash and Pikachu headed back to the Vertress City Pokémon Centre. The friends were in the mood to celebrate – notching up a victory against a rival of Trip's calibre didn't happen every day of the week! Now it was time for Team Ash to rest and recuperate.

"Nurse Joy will have you feeling better in no time," grinned Ash, patting Pikachu protectively.

"Pika-Pika!" chirruped the Pokémon in reply.

Ash strolled up to the reception desk. There was Trip! It looked as though the Trainer was checking out.

"Are you leaving already?" asked Ash.

Trip nodded firmly. "You won it fair and square, but next time will be different. If I'm ever going to defeat Alder, I'll have to be stronger than I am now."

Ash tried to argue with Trip, but his mind was made up.

"That's just the way it is," he insisted, grabbing his bag and making towards the door.

"All right!" agreed Ash. "So let's both give it our best!"

Trip looked on in surprise. Ash, his archrival, was reaching out to shake hands! He paused for a moment, then held out his hand, too. For a moment the pair forgot about their conflicts – they were just two Trainers showing mutual respect.

Trip chuckled, then waved goodbye. It was time for his journey to continue elsewhere. Ash wished him well. Although they were enemies in the Battle Gym, who said that they couldn't be friendly outside it? The pair had a lot in common after all!

That evening, Ash and Cilan decided to take a sauna. It was just the kind of therapy that Ash needed – he had to stay in tip-top form if he was going to make it through the next round of the Unova League!

"Pikachu battled like a total champion back there!" beamed Ash.

"It was a battle that showcased the perfect blend of Pokémon and Trainer," corrected Cilan. "Bravo!"

Just then two more guys muscled into the sauna.

"Nice and hot!" grinned Stephan.

Cameron nodded. "We'll work up a good sweat in no time!"

Ash budged up so that his friends could sit down. Stephan and Cameron were delighted to see their Trainer buddy... and hear the inside story on how he beat Trip.

"Fantastic work! How did you pull it off?" asked Cameron. "I've got to know!"

Ash wiped the sweat off his brow. With Stephan and Cameron huddled up next to him there was hardly room to breathe!

"It's getting a little hot in here," he gasped.

No duh! Cameron and Stephan both giggled.

"That's 'cause it's a sauna!"

Downstairs, the Trainers' Pokémon were also making the most of the facilities. They were having a fine old time in the hot springs!

"Osha-wott..."

Oshawott floated happily in the pool while Pikachu and Riolu splashed each other playfully on the other side. The splashing got harder and harder until...

"PIKA-CHU!"

Riolu had splattered its friend one time too many. Pikachu blew a fuse! The feisty Pokémon sparked with electricity, then blasted the pool with all his might. Riolu dodged the bolt, but Oshawott wasn't quite so lucky. The unfortunate Pokémon learned the hard way that water and electricity don't mix!

Ash grabbed his towel and headed out to the rest room. It was time to cool off!

"There's nothing like Moomoo Milk after a sauna," smiled Cameron, glugging down a bottle.

"Ice-cold Soda Pop's good, too!" pipped up Stephan.

But when the Trainers headed down to check on their Pokémon, they were in for a nasty shock. Pikachu and Riolu were in good shape, but poor Oshawott had endured an electrifying experience!

"What happened here?" cried Ash.

The unlucky Pokémon was still floating in the water, sparking from ears to tail. Ash groaned – trust Pikachu and his pals to get up to mischief!

The next morning, everybody was up bright and early. It was time for another thrilling round of the Vertress City Unova League! Freddy the Scoop was on hand to announce the first round match-ups.

"First round Trainers will use two Pokémon each," he explained, before adding, "and substitutions are allowed!"

The crowds gazed at the big screen as the contestants' names flashed up in turn. Trainers waited breathlessly. What would the match-ups be?

"Our first battle will be… Cameron versus Bianca!"

The crowd went wild! Ash couldn't believe it – two of his friends were going head to head already!

"So which one am I going to cheer for?" mumbled Stephan.

Cilan, Iris and Axew made their way to their seats.

"Here we go!" remarked Cilan. "I wonder how this is going to turn out?"

Iris clapped her hands in anticipation. She couldn't wait to see!

Cameron looked nervously at his friend Riolu – it was show time! The Trainer wondered which Pokémon would be best to give Bianca a run for her money.

The judge called for silence, then signalled the beginning of the battle.

"All right, Samurott," decided Cameron. "Let's go!"

The Water-type loomed into view. The sword in its impressive armour glinted menacingly in the light. Samurott would be a tricky foe to beat!

"OK," smiled Bianca. "Come on out, Escavalier!"

Quick as a flash, Samurott went in with Hydro Cannon, pummelling Escavalier with all its might. Luckily Bianca was ready, using Iron Defence not once, but twice. Freddy the Scoop was impressed – using Iron Defence twice would really raise Escavalier's defence power!

"Use Razor Shell!" urged Cameron, getting frustrated.

"Iron Defence!" retorted Bianca.

Iron Defence again? Ash frowned. Bianca needed to be more aggressive then this!

"Using Iron Defence any more won't make its defence any stronger," sighed Cilan.

Luckily Bianca had a few more tricks up her sleeve. The crowd fell quiet as Escavalier pulled off an awesome Fury Attack. Now it was Samurott's turn to focus on standing strong!

"Samurott's showing some impressive defence as well," remarked Freddy.

Cameron's mind was racing – he had to find his opponent's weak point! Everyone could see that Escavalier's armour was holding out well on the outside, but would it work against shockwaves inside?

"Hit hard with a double Razor Shell!"

Samurott unleashed its full force, inflicting a powerful hit on its rival. Bianca was unfazed – Escavalier's armour seemed to absorb the blow completely! Soon however, the damage started to take its toll.

"It looks like something's wrong with Escavalier!" cried Iris.

Thud!

Bianca's brave Pokémon collapsed on the floor. Escavalier was unable to battle!

"Pretty good," conceded Bianca, summoning Escavalier to its Poké Ball. "Next up I'm going to use Emboar!"

Ash and his friends were amazed. There was no doubt that Emboar was an impressive Pokémon, but this kind of Fire-type was bound to be at a disadvantage against a Water-type like Samurott! Cilan hoped that Bianca had a strategy in mind.

"Let's wrap this up!" announced Cameron. "Now Samurott, Aqua Jet!"

Emboar braced itself against an inevitable jet of water. Samurott followed the attack up with a merciless Hydro Cannon – Emboar seemed to be helpless against its powerful Water-type's moves.

"I was hoping to see Riolu battle," groaned Ash, "but the odds don't look so good."

Stephan and Pikachu had to agree. Bianca's decision to use Emboar seemed set to take her out of the Unova League.

"I've had enough of this!" yelled Cameron, sending Samurott in with another attack. "Let's get it over with!"

Bianca should have been panicking, but instead she broke into a knowing smile.

"All right, Emboar," she urged. "Use Attract!"

Ash gasped as hearts revolved around Bianca's Pokémon. Being a female, Samurott had no resistance, quickly falling under Emboar's spell.

"So that's why Bianca chose Emboar!" said Stephan.

"Now it's the perfect time for Arm Thrust!" piped up Bianca.

Emboar powered forward, following up with Hammer Arm. This was Samurott's cue to escape, but the Pokémon was utterly entranced. Instead of dodging its enemy's blows it stood fixed to the floor.

"Dodge it, Samurott!" wailed Cameron.

Too late. In a surge of power, Emboar felled Samurott in a single blow.

"Samurott is unable to battle," announced the judge. "Emboar wins!"

"Yippee!" squealed Bianca.

Ash and his friends cheered. Bianca's performance had knocked Cameron out of the park!

"I'd say we have ourselves a brand new battle!" beamed Cilan.

It was the last stage in a super-tense encounter. Cameron knew exactly who to combat with this time around…

"Cameron has chosen Riolu," said Freddy over the loudspeaker. "Now both competitors are using their second Pokémon."

Iris and Cilan were intrigued. Would Riolu be able to handle a big and powerful opponent like Emboar? Bianca, however, looked dismayed with Cameron's choice.

"Riolu's such a cutie!" she whispered to herself. "How am I going to battle against such an adorable Pokémon?"

"Give it all you've got!" urged Cameron.

Bianca dug deep, then replied to Cameron's battle cry with Emboar's formidable Arm Thrust move!

"Riolu, Dodge!" shouted Cameron, just in the nick of time.

Riolu was small, but it was nimble, too. The Pokémon skillfully evaded every attack before pulling off a Circle Throw that sent Emboar crashing to the ground.

"Finesse over brute strength," gushed Freddy the Scoop.

"Ample power in small size," agreed Cilan. "Riolu deserves much respect!"

The crowd watched transfixed as the opponents exchanged thunderous blows. The advantage went this way and that, until Emboar used its epic Flamethrower move.

"Use Copycat!" cried Cameron.

Ash couldn't believe his eyes. Riolu dodged Emboar then began to glow with heat. Copycat allowed the Pokémon to duplicate its rival's last move with devastating effect. Seizing the moment, Cameron followed up with a Vacuum Wave.

Bianca gasped. Emboar was knocked out cold! Cameron and Riolu had won the battle and the match. The friends grasped each other in a tight victory hug.

"Cameron's trained Riolu really well," beamed Stephan.

"You bet!" nodded Ash. "I can't wait to battle them both!"

Cameron wins the first match of the day with an exciting triumph over Bianca. Could this be a sign of great things to come in Vertress City?

SERPERIOR SPOT

Trip's Serperior makes a formidable opponent! Study these images of the Grass-type in action. Only two match exactly. Are you sharp enough to spot them?

A

B

C

D

E

F

G

H

I

THE ANSWERS ARE WAITING ON PAGE 76

TRAINING TEST

When you're on a quest to win the Unova League, your mind is in the game 24/7! Ash wants to put in some extra hours refining his battle skills. Another talented Trainer has agreed to practise with him. Can you work out who it is?

Read the clues, then use your knowledge to eliminate the possible rivals from the list. Ash will take on the last name left. Good luck!

CLUE 1
The Trainer is male.

CLUE 2
The Trainer has made it through to the third round of the Unova League.

CLUE 3
The Trainer often uses a Fighting-type Pokémon.

CLUE 4
The Trainer likes to sleep in a tent at night.

STEPHAN

CAMERON

BIANCA

VIRGIL

TRIP

Finding it tough? Flip to the story pages – they're packed full of Trainer info from the Unova League!

AXEW

TYPE: Dragon
CATEGORY: Tusk
HEIGHT: 0.6m   WEIGHT: 18.0kg

Axew uses its tusks to crush Berries for food and cut gashes in trees to mark its territory. Its tusks are sharp because they grow constantly.

DRUDDIGON

TYPE: Dragon
CATEGORY: Cave
HEIGHT: 1.6m   WEIGHT: 139.0kg

The skin on Druddigon's face is harder than rock, and it speeds through narrow caves to catch prey in its sharp claws. Its wings absorb sunlight.

FRAXURE

TYPE: Dragon
CATEGORY: Axe Jaw
HEIGHT: 1.0m   WEIGHT: 36.0kg

Fraxure's tusks can shatter rock, and the fights can get violent against other Fraxures. It carefully sharpens its tusks on river rocks after battling.

HAXORUS

TYPE: Dragon
CATEGORY: Axe Jaw
HEIGHT: 1.8m   WEIGHT: 105.5kg

Haxorus may be kind, but it is relentless when defending territory. It challenges foes with tusks sturdy enough to cut through steel.

KYUREM

TYPE: Dragon-Ice
CATEGORY: Boundary
HEIGHT: 3.0m   WEIGHT: 325.0kg

Able to create ultracold air, Kyurem can generate a powerful, freezing energy. But when this energy leaked out, its body was frozen.

RESHIRAM

TYPE: Dragon-Fire
CATEGORY: Vast White
HEIGHT: 3.2m   WEIGHT: 330.0kg

The flame from Reshiram's tail can sear everything around it, and when that tail flares, the heat stirs the atmosphere and alters weather worldwide.

ZEKROM

TYPE: Dragon-Electric
CATEGORY: Deep Black
HEIGHT: 2.9m   WEIGHT: 345.0kg

Spoken of in ancient stories, Zekrom flies across Unova, hidden by thunderclouds. Its tail contains a massive generator that creates electricity.

BLITZLE

TYPE: Electric
CATEGORY: Electrified
HEIGHT: 0.8m   WEIGHT: 29.8kg

When the sky is covered in thunderclouds, Blitzle appears. It communicates with other Blitzle by flashing its mane, which shines when it discharges electricity.

EELEKTRIK

TYPE: Electric
CATEGORY: EleFish
HEIGHT: 1.2m   WEIGHT: 22.0kg

Eelektrik has a big appetite. Once it sees prey, it attacks, using electricity. The circular patterns on its body are electricity-generating organs.

EELEKTROSS

TYPE: Electric
CATEGORY: EleFish
HEIGHT: 2.1m   WEIGHT: 80.5kg

Eelektross can attack prey on shore and drag it into the ocean. Once its draws the target into its sucker mouth, it shocks its prey with electricity.

EMOLGA

TYPE: Electric-Flying
CATEGORY: Sky Squirrel
HEIGHT: 0.4m   WEIGHT: 5.0kg

This treetop-dwelling Pokémon generates electricity in its cheeks and stores it in a cape-like membrane. It can glide using the inner surface of the membrane.

THUNDURUS

TYPE: Electric-Flying
CATEGORY: Bolt Strike
HEIGHT: 1.5m   WEIGHT: 61.0kg

Thundurus flies through the Unova region, firing huge lightning bolts from the spikes on its tail and leaving charred landscapes in its wake.

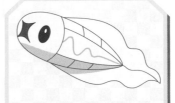

TYNAMO

TYPE: Electric
CATEGORY: EleFish
HEIGHT: 0.2m   WEIGHT: 0.3kg

Tynamo releases electricity if threatened. A single Tynamo doesn't have much power, but a large group can be as powerful as lightning.

ZEBSTRIKA

TYPE: Electric
CATEGORY: Thunderbolt
HEIGHT: 1.6m   WEIGHT: 79.5kg

Zebstrika moves like lightning and echoes like thunder when it runs at top speed. Whenever it gets angry, lightning shoots from its mane in all directions.

CONKELDURR

TYPE: Fighting
CATEGORY: Muscular
HEIGHT: 1.4m WEIGHT: 87.0kg

Conkeldurr swings its concrete pillars around when in battle. It taught humans how to make concrete over 2,000 years ago, or so it's been said.

GURDURR

TYPE: Fighting
CATEGORY: Muscular
HEIGHT: 1.2m WEIGHT: 40.0kg

Gurdurr is so muscular and strong, a team of wrestlers couldn't budge it one bit. It carries around steel beams to make itself even stronger.

MIENFOO

TYPE: Fighting
CATEGORY: Martial Arts
HEIGHT: 0.9m WEIGHT: 20.0kg

This Pokémon has mastered elegant combos, dominating battles with flowing attacks. By concentrating, Mienfoo makes its moves even faster and more precise.

MIENSHAO

TYPE: Fighting
CATEGORY: Martial Arts
HEIGHT: 1.4m WEIGHT: 35.5kg

Mienshao wields the long fur on its arms like a whip, unleashing attacks too fast to see.

SAWK

TYPE: Fighting
CATEGORY: Karate
HEIGHT: 1.4m WEIGHT: 51.0kg

When Sawk trains in the mountains, the sound of its punches hitting boulders and trees can be heard far away. If its training is disturbed, it gets angry!

THROH

TYPE: Fighting
CATEGORY: Judo
HEIGHT: 1.3m WEIGHT: 55.5kg

A Throh tries to heave any foe that's larger than itself, always travelling in a pack of five. A wild Throh weaves its belt out of vines.

TIMBURR

TYPE: Fighting
CATEGORY: Muscular
HEIGHT: 0.6m WEIGHT: 12.5kg

Timburr shows up at construction sites and helps with the work. It always carries a squared-off log that it can swing like a weapon.

DARMANITAN

TYPE: Fire
CATEGORY: Blazing
HEIGHT: 1.3m WEIGHT: 92.9kg

If weakened, Darmanitan becomes motionless as a stone and resorts to psychic attacks instead. It is powered by an internal fire that burns at 2,500° F.

DARUMAKA

TYPE: Fire
CATEGORY: Zen Charm
HEIGHT: 0.6m WEIGHT: 37.5kg

Its droppings are hot, so people used to stay warm by tucking Darumaka droppings inside their clothing. When its internal fire goes down, it sleeps.

EMBOAR

TYPE: Fire-Fighting
CATEGORY: Mega Fire Pig
HEIGHT: 1.6m WEIGHT: 150.0kg

Emboar is loyal to its friends and adept at powerful fighting moves. It grows a fiery beard, and can set its fists aflame for a blazing punch.

HEATMOR

TYPE: Fire
CATEGORY: Anteater
HEIGHT: 1.4m WEIGHT: 58.0kg

Heatmor has an internal flame and uses a hole in its tail to breathe. Its searing, fiery tongue can pierce the armour of its main prey, Durant.

PANSEAR

TYPE: Fire
CATEGORY: High Temp
HEIGHT: 0.6m WEIGHT: 11.0kg

Pansear lives in volcanic caverns and uses the tuft on its head to roast Berries. The inside of this tuft burns hotter if Pansear gets angry.

PIGNITE

TYPE: Fire-Fighting
CATEGORY: Fire Pig
HEIGHT: 1.0m WEIGHT: 55.5kg

Anything it eats becomes fuel for the fire in its stomach. This fire burns hottest when Pignite is angry, making its moves faster and sharper.

SIMISEAR

TYPE: Fire
CATEGORY: Ember
HEIGHT: 1.0m WEIGHT: 28.0kg

Simisear has a taste for sweets, which fuel the fire inside it. It burns foes by scattering embers from its head and tail.

TEPIG

TYPE: Fire
CATEGORY: Fire Pig
HEIGHT: 0.5m WEIGHT: 9.9kg

Tepig can blow fire from its nose, either to launch fireballs or to roast Berries for food. But if it catches a cold, it blows out black smoke instead.

TORNADUS

TYPE: Flying
CATEGORY: Cyclone
HEIGHT: 1.5m WEIGHT: 63.0kg

With its lower half shrouded in a cloud of energy, Tornadus zooms through the air. It can create powerful storms with the energy expelled from its tail.

SHATTERED

Uh-oh! This Pokédex has been dropped during the heat of an encounter. Now the screen has shattered, making it impossible to read properly. Can you find the right pieces to fill the gaps in the glass?

write the correct letter next to each numbered space.

FLAME GAME

Despite its defeat against Cameron's Riolu, no one can deny that Bianca's Emboar is hot stuff! Is your Fire-type knowledge smokin', too? Let's see...

This crossword is all about Fire-type Pokémon. Take a flick through the Pokédex pages on 30-31, then use the facts and profiles to help you answer each and every clue.

DOWN

1. The part of the body where Pignite's fire burns.

2. Tepig's next Evolution.

3. The Fire-type that is known for leaving hot droppings.

4. The colour of Tepig's snout.

5. The illness that makes Tepig blow black smoke from its nose.

ACROSS

1. A Fire-type with a bushy red tail and a taste for sweets.

2. Pansear's mood when its tuft burns the fiercest.

3. A Pokémon that breathes through a hole in its tail.

4. One of the three options for a beginning Trainer's first Pokémon in Unova.

5. The flamy growth that covers Emboar's chin.

PERFECT MATCH

Choosing Pokémon is no easy business – Trainers need to capture species that suit their personality and battle style.
All of the Unova Pokémon on this page have played a part in the contest at Vertress City, pulling out some knockout moves when their Trainers needed it most. Look down each column, then name the Pokémon hiding on this page. Can you score three out of three?

A

A diminutive Water-type with a wide paddle tail

An option for a beginning Trainer's first Pokémon in Unova

Has a detachable scalchop on its belly

Ash battles with it

__ __ __ __ __ __ __

B

A courageous adversary that wears a Shelmet's shell

Has two pointed spears

Known as the Cavalry Pokémon

Bianca battles with it

__ __ __ __ __ __ __ __ __

C

The evolved form of Dewott.

An impressive Pokémon with a pointed horn

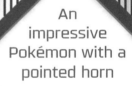

Can silence foes with a single glare

Cameron battles with it

__ __ __ __ __ __ __ __

A ROUTE FOR RIOLU

Riolu might be small, but it sure packs a mean punch! It is new to the Unova region so the local Fighting-types have turned out to show it around. Use their Pokémon key to help Riolu find the way to its battle with Emboar.

RIGHT **LEFT** **UP** **DOWN**

START

FINISH

CHANDELURE

TYPE: Ghost-Fire
CATEGORY: Luring
HEIGHT: 1.0m WEIGHT: 34.3kg

Chandelure's flames will consume a spirit, which Chandelure absorbs as fuel. It waves the flames on its arms to hypnotise foes.

COFAGRIGUS

TYPE: Ghost
CATEGORY: Coffin
HEIGHT: 1.7m WEIGHT: 76.5kg

Cofagrigus's body is covered in pure gold, and it poses as an ornate coffin to punish grave robbers. It likes to eat gold nuggets.

LAMPENT

TYPE: Ghost-Fire
CATEGORY: Lamp
HEIGHT: 0.6m WEIGHT: 13.0kg

People fear this ominous Pokémon, which searches through cities for spirits of the fallen. Lampent can even steal the spirit out of a body.

LITWICK

TYPE: Ghost-Fire
CATEGORY: Candle
HEIGHT: 0.3m WEIGHT: 3.1kg

Litwick fuels its light with the life energy it absorbs from people and Pokémon. It only pretends to guide others with this light.

YAMASK

TYPE: Ghost
CATEGORY: Spirit
HEIGHT: 0.5m WEIGHT: 1.5kg

Yamask comes from the spirit of a person from the ancient past. It holds a mask of the face it had when it was human.

AMOONGUSS

TYPE: Grass-Poison
CATEGORY: Mushroom
HEIGHT: 0.6m WEIGHT: 10.5kg

To lure prey, Amoonguss dances and waves its Poké-Ball-like arm caps in a swaying motion. Not many Pokémon are fooled.

COTTONEE

TYPE: Grass
CATEGORY: Cotton Puff
HEIGHT: 0.3m WEIGHT: 0.6kg

Cottonee travels on the winds, sheltering beneath large trees on rainy days when its body becomes heavier. If attacked, it shoots cotton from its body.

FERROSEED

TYPE: Grass-Steel
CATEGORY: Thorn Seed
HEIGHT: 0.6m WEIGHT: 18.8kg

By sticking its spikes into a cave wall, Ferroseed absorbs minerals from the rock. When in danger, it shoots a barrage of spikes and rolls away.

FERROTHORN

TYPE: Grass-Steel
CATEGORY: Thorn Pod
HEIGHT: 1.0m WEIGHT: 110.0kg

Ferrothorn attaches itself to the ceiling of a cave and fires steel spikes at targets passing below. It also fights by swinging its three spiked feelers.

FOONGUS

TYPE: Grass-Poison
CATEGORY: Mushroom
HEIGHT: 0.2m WEIGHT: 1.0kg

For reasons as yet unknown, this Pokémon looks like a Poké Ball. Foongus uses its pattern to lure people close, then releases poison spores.

LILLIGANT

TYPE: Grass
CATEGORY: Flowering
HEIGHT: 1.1m WEIGHT: 16.3kg

Though Lilligant is popular with celebrities, getting its lovely flower to bloom can prove a challenge. The garland on its head has a relaxing scent.

MARACTUS

TYPE: Grass
CATEGORY: Cactus
HEIGHT: 1.0m WEIGHT: 28.0kg

Maractus moves in rhythm while making a sound like maracas. It does a lively song to ward off avian Pokémon who are after its flower seeds.

PANSAGE

TYPE: Grass
CATEGORY: Grass Monkey
HEIGHT: 0.6m WEIGHT: 10.5kg

Pansage lives deep in the forest. The edible leaf on its head has stress-relieving properties, and Pansage shares this leaf with tired-looking Pokémon.

PETILIL

TYPE: Grass
CATEGORY: Bulb
HEIGHT: 0.5m WEIGHT: 6.6kg

The leaves on Petilil's head are very bitter, but reinvigorate a tired body if eaten. Petilil favors damp, nutrient-rich soil.

SERPERIOR

TYPE: Grass
CATEGORY: Regal
HEIGHT: 3.3m WEIGHT: 63.0kg

Serperior absorbs solar energy and magnifies it. When Serperior rears its head, its glare alone is enough to halt an opponent.

SERVINE

TYPE: Grass
CATEGORY: Grass Snake
HEIGHT: 0.8m WEIGHT: 16.0kg

Servine almost glides across the ground, and foes are baffled by its quick moves. It can slip into the shadow of thick vegetation to avoid attacks.

SIMISAGE

TYPE: Grass
CATEGORY: Thorn Monkey
HEIGHT: 1.1m   WEIGHT: 30.5kg

This short-tempered Pokémon fights with wild swings of its thorn-covered tail. The leaves growing on its head are extremely bitter.

SNIVY

TYPE: Grass
CATEGORY: Grass Snake
HEIGHT: 0.6m   WEIGHT: 8.1kg

Calm Snivy speeds up when exposed to lots of sunlight. By bathing its tail in solar rays, it can photosynthesise. If it feels unwell, its tail droops.

VIRIZON

TYPE: Grass-Fighting
CATEGORY: Grassland
HEIGHT: 2.0m   WEIGHT: 200.0kg

Virizion's horns are as sharp as blades. Moving like a whirlwind, it quickly cuts and confounds its opponents. Legends are still told about this Pokémon.

WHIMSICOTT

TYPE: Grass
CATEGORY: Windveiled
HEIGHT: 0.7m   WEIGHT: 6.6kg

Whimsicott rides on whirlwinds and sneaks into houses to cause mischief. Like the wind, it is able to slip through even the smallest crack.

DRILBUR

TYPE: Ground
CATEGORY: Mole
HEIGHT: 0.3m   WEIGHT: 8.5kg

By putting its claws together and spinning at speed, it swiftly burrows through the ground. It can dig fast enough to race a car on the surface.

EXCADRILL

TYPE: Ground-Steel
CATEGORY: Subterrene
HEIGHT: 0.7m   WEIGHT: 40.4kg

Excadrill builds maze-like nests deep underground. It can help with tunnel construction. Its steel drill is hard enough to bore through iron plates.

GOLETT

TYPE: Ground-Ghost
CATEGORY: Automaton
HEIGHT: 1.0m   WEIGHT: 92.0kg

It's thought that Golett was created by the science of a mysterious ancient civilization. No one has yet identified the energy that enables it to move.

GOLURK

TYPE: Ground-Ghost
CATEGORY: Automaton
HEIGHT: 2.8m   WEIGHT: 330.0kg

Stories say that an ancient people created Golurk. It flies at Mach speeds but it goes haywire if the seal on its chest is removed.

KROKOROK

TYPE: Ground-Dark
CATEGORY: Desert Croc
HEIGHT: 1.0m   WEIGHT: 33.4kg

A protective membrane shields Krokorok's eyes from sandstorms. This membrane also senses heat, enabling Krokorok to see in the dark.

KROOKODILE

TYPE: Ground-Dark
CATEGORY: Intimidation
HEIGHT: 1.5m   WEIGHT: 96.3kg

Krookodile never lets prey get away. It has jaws powerful enough to crush a car body and eyes like binoculars, able to see faraway objects.

LANDORUS

TYPE: Ground-Flying
CATEGORY: Abundance
HEIGHT: 1.5m   WEIGHT: 68.0kg

Landorus is hailed as "The Guardian of the Fields" because wherever it goes, a bountiful crop follows. Energy pours from its tail and fertilises the soil.

SANDILE

TYPE: Ground-Dark
CATEGORY: Desert Croc
HEIGHT: 0.7m   WEIGHT: 15.2kg

Sandile lives buried in the warm sand keeping its body temperature from dropping. Only its nose and eyes are exposed — a membrane protects its eyes.

STUNFISK

TYPE: Ground-Electric
CATEGORY: Trap
HEIGHT: 0.7m   WEIGHT: 11.0kg

Stunfisk's skin is incredibly hard. Hidden in mud along the seashore, Stunfisk waits for prey to make contact, then gives off an electrical jolt.

RECIPE FOR SUCCESS

When it comes to putting together winning combinations, one name stands out from the crowd! Who do Ash and Iris turn to when they need advice on building the crucial bond between Trainer and Pokémon?

There's an A-class Pokémon Connoisseur hidden in this letter grid. Find a pen, then cross out all of the letters that appear in the box more than once. Next rearrange the ones that are left to reveal the right answer.

F	F	P	K	F	G	N	K	D	Z
M	B	H	D	P	Z	B	T	R	H
Y	V	R	U	K	E	U	M	E	O
F	P	S	A	W	G	W	K	R	Z
O	M	F	H	Y	Y	D	H	P	C
Z	D	J	G	E	X	J	R	J	W
X	T	Q	K	V	B	V	F	K	P
V	G	E	O	J	S	H	V	T	P
G	B	S	D	M	G	D	K	B	H
X	O	I	O	J	Q	F	W	L	E

ANSWER:

THE SCOOP FROM FREDDY

Freddy the Scoop is Unova's top announcer! From the opening ceremony right through to the final battle blow, Freddy has his microphone switched on and ready to commentate on all the action.

Think you'd make a good Pokémon pundit? Let's find out! Use the missing words at the bottom of the page to fill in the blanks in Freddy's sentences.

1

From .... to Wrap, Serperior's powerful combination scores a huge hit!

2

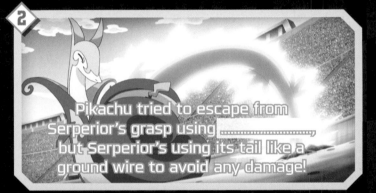

Pikachu tried to escape from Serperior's grasp using ...., but Serperior's using its tail like a ground wire to avoid any damage!

3

The victories are piling up one after another here at the .... stadium!

4

.... has freed itself by smashing into the field with Iron Tail!

5

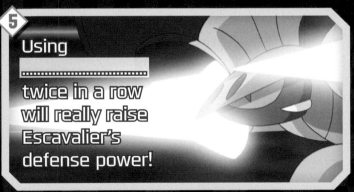

Using .... twice in a row will really raise Escavalier's defense power!

6

As a Fire-type, Emboar seems to be helpless against the onslaught of Samurott's powerful .... moves!

THUNDERBOLT   DRAGON TAIL   UNOVA LEAGUE
PIKACHU   IRON DEFENSE   WATER-TYPE

LOST AT THE LEAGUE!

After his dazzling defeat of Trip, Ash is ready to take his challenge further in the Unova League! Can Ash's Scraggy secure him a coveted place in the third round? Only our hero can decide!

Ash gave his Scraggy an encouraging nod – this second round battle against Darumaka was reaching a breathtaking climax!

At just the right moment, the rubbery-skinned Pokémon launched itself headfirst into one final attack. Up in the commentary tower, Freddy the Scoop nodded in admiration.

"There's Scraggy's flashy yet graceful Hi Jump Kick!"

Darumaka was floored. Its Trainer sank to his knees, urging the Fire-type to get back up, but Ash sent Scraggy in to finish the job with a Headbutt.

"Darumaka is unable to battle!" confirmed the judge. "Scraggy wins! Which means, the winner is Ash!"

Ash punched the air – he was through to the third round!

"Spectacular back-to-back battles!" announced Freddy, as the other round winners flashed up on the screen. Cilan, Iris and Bianca cheered and clapped. Stephan, Cameron and Virgil had all made it through, too!

Ash and fifteen other skilled Trainers had earned themselves places in the tournament's top sixteen.

"I can hardly wait to find out who they'll all be battling against next!" gushed Bianca.

Right on cue, Freddy the Scoop stepped back up to the commentary mic.

"And now, time to announce the match-ups for the third round. Ladies and gentlemen, please turn your attention to the big screen."

Every spectator in the Vertress City arena waited in hushed silence. One by one the Trainer pairings flashed up. Ash scanned the monitor for his photo. He gasped in surprise – he had been matched up with Stephan!

"The excitement begins first thing tomorrow morning," continued Freddy. "Rest up and prepare yourself for another dose of red-hot battle action!"

Competing in the third round was going to be tough, but first it was time for some rest and relaxation. Cilan, Bianca and Iris thought they'd start with a stroll.

"The third round is all three-on-three matches!" remarked Cilan. "Ash and Stephan know each other well, so I'm sure that they're having a hard time deciding which Pokémon to use."

Suddenly Bianca let out a tingling shriek. She'd just spotted a poster for her favourite ice cream!

"I forgot Casteliacones are going on sale today!" she cried.

Iris shrugged. "Excuse me, but we're in Vertress City?

Cilan explained that lots of famous places from around the Unova region set up shop here during the tournament – it was the perfect way to add some additional spice to the league!

Bianca didn't hang around a second longer. She'd already run off to bite into a Casteliacone!

"Why don't we go check out the shop later, too?" smiled Iris.

Across the hall, Ash and Stephan were looking forward to the next round.

"I'm not holding back," promised Ash.

"Took the words right out of my mouth," countered Stephan. "May the best Trainer win!"

"You bet!"

Cameron however, didn't seem quite as focussed on the challenge ahead.

"All packed and ready to go," he said to his Riolu. "I'll be there first, then the very best spot will be mine all mine!"

"You going somewhere?" asked Ash.

Cameron looked pityingly on his pals. They were totally clueless!

"Today is Fireworks Day!" he replied. "It's a celebration! Flashy fireworks for the tournament! I'm gonna find the best place to watch them!"

Ash glanced at Pikachu. Fireworks did sound like a lot of fun.

"I'd rather stay and hit the sauna," decided Stephan. "Time for me to build up a good strategy sweat."

Ash waved goodbye to the Trainers, then turned to greet Iris and Cilan.

"Wow, Ash you did it!" grinned Iris. "Good luck in the third round."

Ash smiled proudly. Scraggy had been truly awesome in the battle against Darumaka. Cilan was advising the Trainer not to let his guard down when Pikachu alerted the group to a worrying discovery.

"What's up, Pikachu?" asked Ash.

Iris scanned the hallway. Her Axew had disappeared!

While the others had been talking strategy, Axew had been distracted by a floating red balloon. The bold little Dragon-type scuttled down the corridor, straight into a visiting fan club! The group were huddled excitedly around a young Trainer called Russet.

"Russet is in the third round!" announced the club's delighted leader. "This is the first time a Trainer from our little town has gotten this far in the Unova League. Today is declared 'Celebrate Russet Day'!"

Axew peeped up at a lady called Selma.

"You want to celebrate with us?" she chuckled. "What a darling!"

Poor Axew found itself being dressed up in a party hat and bow tie. The partying fan clubbers scooped the Pokémon up and charged outside.

Moments later, Iris arrived on the scene.

"This is weird," she blubbed. "Where did Axew go?"

"It's possible that Axew went back to the dormitory," suggested Cilan.

Iris shook her head. Her companion would never go back alone.

"Hey guys," said a familiar voice. "Is something the matter?"

Ash gasped. It was Virgil!

In no time at all, Axew found itself in the middle of a victory party. Russet's fan club stampeded through the centre of Vertress City, searching for places to eat.

"It's a party," insisted the club's president, "and you can't have a party without food!"

The group made a beeline for the nearest market stall. Russet's supporters were so keen to chow down, they didn't notice when Axew gave them the slip. The bemused Pokémon leant against a drinks stand to catch its breath. Suddenly the owner thrust a bottle into its paw.

"Try our famous soda pop," he said brightly. "It will make you happy!"

Axew blinked. These visiting storeowners were certainly a generous bunch! Opposite, a lady emerged carrying a box of apples.

"You can have these if you like," she smiled, handing the fruit to a passing Garbodor. "Share them with friends!"

Garbodor took the apples gratefully, then shuffled round the corner. Axew watched four little Trubbish emerge from the shadows.

"Garbodor!"

The kindly Pokémon shared out the feast.

Iris, meanwhile, was getting seriously worried. She and her Axew were usually inseparable! Virgil suggested that they checked the security team's CCTV footage. The surveillance camera footage was sure to throw up something!

Soon the clever pals were staring up at a dozen black and white TV screens.

"It doesn't make sense that Axew would just disappear," muttered Ash.

Cilan clapped his hands with glee. He loved playing detective!

"Every mystery is begging to be solved," he insisted. "There's only one person present who is perfect for the job... me!"

Iris frowned. Cilan's constant chatter was ruining her concentration!

"Hold on!" she shouted. "Play that part again one more time."

The gang moved closer to the screen. Iris freeze-framed on Axew. The Pokémon seemed to be part of a group heading towards the city centre.

Ash didn't want to waste another second.

"Let's go, Iris!"

On another side of the market, Bianca found a bench in the sun. She wanted to savour every slurp of her gourmet ice cream!

"Casteliacones are the best!" she squealed. "I'm giddy!"

Before she could take another scrummy lick Axew tottered past, sipping on a soda pop.

"Oh!" gasped Bianca, taking in the crazy outfit. "That hat looks so cute on you!"

Axew beamed. It rushed up to greet the Trainer... and was swept up by Russet's fan club again! The over-eager group had set their sights on another snack stall.

"Frozen delicacies direct from Driftveil market!" guffawed the president. "Let's eat them all!"

Bianca rubbed her eyes. Axew had disappeared again. Did that really just happen?

Down by the lake, Cameron had found the perfect camping spot. He put up his tent and got ready to make the most of the display.

"That should do it," the Trainer told his Riolu. "Now bring on those fireworks!"

A commotion rumbled in the distance. The rumble got louder and louder, until Russet's fan club thundered into view with Axew still in tow! The determined partygoers stampeded past Cameron and Riolu.

When they had gone, Cameron took in the damage.

"You can't be serious!" he yelled. The tent was trampled into the ground!

By the time Iris, got into town, the runaway Pokémon was long gone.

"Axew, where are you?" Iris called. "Answer me!"

Just then Bianca picked her way through the crowd, armed with a very special gift.

"I brought you some Casteliacones! Wait until..." Kerrang!

Before she could hand over the goodies, Bianca tripped on an empty drink can. The hapless Trainer stumbled into Ash, knocking him into a fountain. Pikachu jumped off his shoulder just before the soaking.

"Uuggh!" groaned Ash. "I am so through with this!"

Poor Axew was having a bewildering time at the party. Russet's fan club were busy tucking into a massive feast. The president led the toasts and tributes.

"Here's to our hometown hero Russet's next Unova League victory," he called enthusiastically.

The revels were getting more and riotous, but Selma noticed that Axew had hardly touched its bowl.

"Don't be shy," she urged, pushing the food a little closer.

Axew gazed helplessly across the lake. A little further along the grass, a young girl was gently feeding her Lillipup.

"Is it good?" she asked tenderly.

The girl reminded Axew of someone very special – Iris! When the Dragon-type was certain that Selma wasn't looking, the Pokémon fled. Axew was desperate to be reunited with its best friend.

The team decided to split up. Pikachu, Scraggy, Oshawott and Emolga searched the side streets, questioning any Pokémon they came across.

"Osha-WOTT!"

Oshawott turned into the alley where the Trubbish family had been playing minutes earlier. Their box of apples sat unguarded in the half-light, still full to the brim.

Oshawott couldn't help itself. It tipped up the box and gobbled down every piece of shiny red fruit. Afterwards it slumped down for a doze, clutching its bloated tummy.

Back in the city, Ash decided to call in some reinforcements. Ash summoned Scraggy and Oshawott, while Iris brought out Emolga. With these loyal Pokémon on the job, they had to find Axew sometime soon!

Bianca tried to remember which way she'd seen the Axew go.

A little later, Garbodor returned to the alley behind the shops. It had found some red balloons for the Trubbish to play with.
"Garbodor?"
Instead of finding four happy Poison-types, the Trubbish sat crying amongst dozens of chewed out apple cores.
Garbodor let go of its balloons. Someone would be punished for this!

Down at the lake, Cameron had finally got his tent back up.
"We're back in shape and as good as new!" he declared, high-fiving with Riolu.
Suddenly Iris swept into view, closely followed by Ash and Cilan. She reached forward to pluck off the party hat that Cameron had balanced on the centre pole.
"That's definitely the hat that Axew was wearing!" she cried.
Cameron's creation collapsed in a sorry heap.
"Why did you wreck my tent?" sobbed the unfortunate Trainer.
Iris had more important things on her mind than camping. Once she'd heard that Axew had indeed passed by, the friends hurried away. Cameron wailed. If they wanted to see the fireworks, he and Riolu were going to have to start all over again. What was it with those guys?

A little further on, poor Axew was feeling more alone than ever. The frightened Pokémon huddled amongst the trees, wondering what to do next.
"Emolga!"

Axew's face lit up. Emolga, Pikachu, Oshawott and Scraggy had come to the rescue! The Pokémon hugged each other and chirruped happily, until a shadow fell across the ground.
Oshawott gulped. Garbodor loomed into view, with four tiny Trubbish peeping out from its feet. Garbodor roared a warning cry. It was time for revenge!

"A ribbon!"
Just a few yards away, Iris bent down to pluck a golden bow off the ground. She recognized it instantly as the one Axew was wearing on the CCTV footage.
"This would indicate Axew's is close by," agreed Cilan.

Bianca buddied up with Virgil. The pair roamed the streets of Vertress City, hoping to unearth a clue about what had happened to Iris's Pokémon.
"We've got to find Axew," she wailed.
Virgil looked up at the sky. They needed to hurry – it wasn't long before nightfall. Just then, a worried looking lady walked past, wringing her hands. She had lost something, too!
"There are four Trubbish living with a Garbodor right down this alleyway," she explained. "They're all suddenly gone!"
The lady shared her theory on who was to blame.
"There was an impertinent looking Oshawott roaming around here with a Pikachu and an Emolga," she went on. "They were up to something!"
Bianca caught Virgil's eye. They'd discovered their first clue!

Up until now Oshawott hadn't realised the trouble he'd caused, but after another blistering attack it finally recognized the advancing Trubbish. It thought back to all the apples it had gorged on, wishing it hadn't been quite so greedy.
Crack!
Oshawott used its scalchop to deflect the first blow, but Garbodor was getting stronger and stronger. The Pokémon were in serious trouble!

At the edge of the forest, the Garbodor in question was still in a very bad mood. It had driven Axew and the other Pokémon to the edge of a cliff. Next it started pelting its quarry with a series of fearsome attack moves.
"Pika-CHU!"
Pikachu sparked with anxiety. They wouldn't be able to hold a gigantic Pokémon like Garbodor off for very much longer.

Iris, Cilan and Ash came bursting through the undergrowth.

"Looks like everybody's here!" shouted Ash, taking in the scene.

"Axew!" called Iris. "You're all right!"

The friends' confidence was of course misplaced. Garbodor stepped forward to unleash a stinging Acid Spray Attack. The force sent Pikachu, Scraggy, Oshawott, Axew and Emolga sprawling over the cliff edge. The Pokémon seemed doomed until...

"Espeon, use Psychic!"

Virgil and Bianca appeared just in the nick of time! Iris gasped with relief as Axew and the others were gently lifted through the air and returned to safe ground.

"Oshawott must have been hungry," surmised Virgil, "because it ate all the fruit that was in the box. That's why Garbodor and the Trubbish are so mad."

"Is that the truth?" asked Ash, his cheeks burning with shame.

Poor Oshawott hung its head.

There was only one thing Ash could do – apologise! The plucky Trainer walked straight up to Garbodor and the Trubbish.

"I feel bad about this," he said. "Oshawott does, too. We all do!"

"Oshawott?"

The Pokémon timidly tried to say sorry, but Garbodor wasn't listening. Instead it replied with a drubbing Gunk Shot move.

Virgil summoned Umbreon. A deft Shadow Ball quickly detonated the Gunk Shot, buying the Pokémon a few more seconds of safety.

"Please calm down Garbodor," said Virgil, lifting a tiny bell out of his breast pocket. "Listen to this."

The gentle tingling sound worked like a lullaby. Garbodor and the Trubbish seemed to breathe in the entrancing music. Any question of an attack was forgotten.

"A Soothe Bell," cooed Bianca. "it really works!"

Cilan nodded.

"I'd expect no less from a member of the Pokémon Rescue Squad."

Ash didn't have a Soothe Bell, but there was something he could do to make amends – throw a feast for Garbodor and the Trubbish! Cilan whipped up a special menu to for the Pokémon to enjoy. Even Oshawott leant a paw.

"We've got plenty more," exclaimed Iris, "so eat til you're full!"

Afterwards, the friends settled down to enjoy the firework display. The spectacular fountains of colour were just as awesome as Cameron had said they would be! Pokémon battles and cool fireworks – what more could a Trainer ask for?

The Russet fan club sat on the banks of the lake, just across from Ash.

"I hope you shine brightly tomorrow like those fireworks," said the president, "and light up our hearts!"

Russet nodded hopefully. Just like the other 15 contestants, he was determined to give the Unova League his best shot!

"What do you know?"

Selma looked over and recognized Axew cradled in Iris's arms.

"From now on no wandering off alone," whispered Iris. "Thank goodness it turned out all right!"

Axew nestled even closer. There was no way it would get lost ever again!

LIEPARD
THE CRUEL POKÉMON
Well-known for its beauty, Liepard uses the elements of surprise when battling opponents, attacking before they can react.

Back at the Pokémon Centre, Ash checked in with Professor Juniper.

"The third round is a three-on-three battle, isn't it? she said. "I'm ready to send any Pokémon you need!"

The next morning, Ash stepped nervously into the Vertress City arena. His battle with Stephan was the first match of the day.

"Man I am ready to rock!" promised Stephan. "Liepard, go!"

Ash flicked open this Pokédex. With Liepard in the mix, this was set to be an epic encounter!!

It's Ash versus Stephan in what's sure to be a red-hot performance! Find out what battle strategies both rivals have in store as the journey continues...

WHERE'S AXEW?

Iris's Axew has got lots of spirit – one day it hopes to evolve into a mighty Haxorus! Normally Iris and her Pokémon are inseparable, but the wayward Dragon-type has wandered off again. Can you help her find it? Follow the trail back to Axew, answering the quiz questions as you go.

START

WHAT IS SERVINE EVOLVED FROM?

A PACK OF PATRAT ARE HELPING IRIS LOOK FOR AXEW. HOW MANY CAN YOU COUNT AROUND THE TRAIL?

NAME THIS POKÉMON.

MARK A TICK WHEN YOU SPOT TINY SOLOSIS HIDING ALONG THE TRAIL. ☐

WHO IS KNOWN AS THE ELESPIDER?

WHAT DO WATCHOG AND STOUTLAND HAVE IN COMMON?

WHAT COLOUR IS VANILLITE?

REARRANGE THIS POKÉMON NAME.
HLRSILFI

FINISH

AUDINO

TYPE: Normal
CATEGORY: Hearing
HEIGHT: 1.1m   WEIGHT: 31.0kg

Audino can sense a person's emotions by touching them with its feelers and listening to the heartbeat. It senses its environment through faint sounds.

BOUFFALANT

TYPE: Normal
CATEGORY: Bash Buffalo
HEIGHT: 1.6m   WEIGHT: 94.6kg

Bouffalant recklessly charges and headbutts anything. Though it attacks with force, its fur absorbs the damage of even the most violent headbutt.

BRAVIARY

TYPE: Normal-Flying
CATEGORY: Valiant
HEIGHT: 1.5m   WEIGHT: 41.0kg

This brave warrior battles for its friends with no thought for its own safety. The more scars a Braviary has, the more its peers respect it.

CINCCINO

TYPE: Normal
CATEGORY: Scarf
HEIGHT: 0.5m   WEIGHT: 7.5kg

Cinccino's white fur has an amazing texture, and its special oil deflects attacks. This fur also repels dust and prevents static electricity build-up.

DEERLING

TYPE: Normal-Grass
CATEGORY: Season
HEIGHT: 0.6m   WEIGHT: 19.5kg

As the seasons change, so does its fur — people use this as a way to mark the seasons. The color and scent of the fur matches the mountain grass.

HERDIER

TYPE: Normal
CATEGORY: Loyal Dog
HEIGHT: 0.9m   WEIGHT: 14.7kg

For ages, Herdier have helped Trainers raise Pokémon, loyally following Trainers' orders. A Herdier's black fur looks like a cape, but it is actually extremely hard.

LILLIPUP

TYPE: Normal
CATEGORY: Puppy
HEIGHT: 0.4m   WEIGHT: 4.1kg

The long hair around its face makes it sensitive to every slight change in its surroundings. Lillipup is intelligent and will retreat if at a disadvantage.

MINCCINO

TYPE: Normal
CATEGORY: Chinchilla
HEIGHT: 0.4m   WEIGHT: 5.8kg

Always sweeping, always dusting, Minccino likes a tidy habitat and uses its tail as a broom. It also uses its clean tail to rub other Minccino as a greeting.

PATRAT

TYPE: Normal
CATEGORY: Scout
HEIGHT: 0.5m   WEIGHT: 11.6kg

Patrat use their tails to communicate, and they keep watch over their nest in shifts. They grow nervous if there's no lookout. It stores food in cheek pouches.

PIDOVE

TYPE: Normal-Flying
CATEGORY: Tiny Pigeon
HEIGHT: 0.3m   WEIGHT: 2.1kg

This city Pokémon is used to people, and many Pidove flock to parks and plazas. Pidove doesn't always understand complicated commands.

RUFFLET

TYPE: Normal-Flying
CATEGORY: Eaglet
HEIGHT: 0.5m   WEIGHT: 10.5kg

Rufflet bravely and fearlessly challenges any opponent, no matter how powerful, and it grows stronger from frequent battles. It crushes Berries in its talons.

SAWSBUCK

TYPE: Normal-Grass
CATEGORY: Season
HEIGHT: 1.9m   WEIGHT: 92.5kg

People track the changing seasons by looking at Sawsbuck's horns. The plants on its horns vary with the seasons. The leader of a herd has impressive horns.

STOUTLAND

TYPE: Normal
CATEGORY: Big-Hearted
HEIGHT: 1.2m   WEIGHT: 61.0kg

Stoutland's shaggy fur coat shields it from the cold. This wise Pokémon is excellent at rescuing people trapped by mountain blizzards or stranded at sea.

TRANQUILL

TYPE: Normal-Flying
CATEGORY: Wild Pigeon
HEIGHT: 0.6m   WEIGHT: 15.0kg

If Tranquill is separated from its Trainer, it can still find its way back, regardless of distance. Wild Tranquill live deep in the forest.

UNFEZANT

TYPE: Normal-Flying
CATEGORY: Proud
HEIGHT: 1.2m   WEIGHT: 29.0kg

Unfezant won't bond with anyone but its Trainer. A male Unfezant can be recognised by its head plumage, which it swings around to threaten foes.

WATCHOG

TYPE: Normal
CATEGORY: Lookout
HEIGHT: 1.1m   WEIGHT: 27.0kg

Watchog threatens predators by making the pattern on its body shine. If it sees a foe, it raises its tail and spits Berry seeds.

GARBODOR

TYPE: Poison
CATEGORY: Trash Heap
HEIGHT: 1.9m   WEIGHT: 107.3kg

Garbodor absorbs garbage into its body. To take down foes, it holds them fast with its left arm and belches putrid, poisonous gas.

TRUBBISH

TYPE: Poison
CATEGORY: Trash Bag
HEIGHT: 0.6m   WEIGHT: 31.0kg

Trubbish was created from a chemical reaction of industrial waste and rubbish bags. The gas it belches leaves a person unconscious for a week if inhaled.

BEHEEYEM

TYPE: Psychic
CATEGORY: Cerebral
HEIGHT: 1.0m   WEIGHT: 34.5kg

Its psychic power can manipulate a target's memory and even control its brain. It seems to communicate by flashing its three differently-coloured fingers.

DUOSION

TYPE: Psychic
CATEGORY: Mitosis
HEIGHT: 0.6m   WEIGHT: 8.0kg

Duosion's divided brains compel it to try two different things at once. When both two brains think the same thing, Duosion shows its greatest power.

ELGYEM

TYPE: Psychic
CATEGORY: Cerebral
HEIGHT: 0.5m   WEIGHT: 9.0kg

This Pokémon was first seen 50 years ago, when it appeared in the desert. Elgyem uses its strong psychic power to inflict unbearable headaches.

GOTHITA

TYPE: Psychic
CATEGORY: Fixation
HEIGHT: 0.4m   WEIGHT: 5.8kg

Gothita is always staring at something — it closely observes all Trainers and Pokémon. Its ribbon-like feelers boost its psychic power.

GOTHITELLE

TYPE: Psychic
CATEGORY: Astral Body
HEIGHT: 1.5m   WEIGHT: 44.0kg

Gothitelle's psychic power distorts space, revealing starry skies from thousands of light-years away. It can predict the future and even see a Trainer's life span.

GOTHORITA

TYPE: Psychic
CATEGORY: Manipulate
HEIGHT: 0.7m   WEIGHT: 18.0kg

Starlight is the source of its power, and Gothorita marks star positions by using psychic energy to levitate stones. Gothorita's hypnosis can control people.

MUNNA

TYPE: Psychic
CATEGORY: Dream Eater
HEIGHT: 0.6m   WEIGHT: 23.3kg

Munna always floats in the air. It eats the dreams of people and Pokémon, and if a dream is eaten by Munna, the dreamer forgets what it was about.

MUSHARNA

TYPE: Psychic
CATEGORY: Drowsing
HEIGHT: 1.1m   WEIGHT: 60.5kg

The mist from its forehead is filled with the dreams of people and Pokémon. Musharna can create the shapes of things from the dreams it's eaten.

REUNICLUS

TYPE: Psychic
CATEGORY: Multiplying
HEIGHT: 1.0m   WEIGHT: 20.1kg

Reuniclus controls arms with a grip strong enough to crush rock. When it shakes hands with another Reuniclus, a network is created between their brains.

SIGILYPH

TYPE: Psychic-Flying
CATEGORY: Avianoid
HEIGHT: 1.4m   WEIGHT: 14.0kg

Clinging to memories of its time as guardian of an ancient city, a Sigilyph always flies the same route and uses psychic power to attack foes who enter its territory.

SOLOSIS

TYPE: Psychic
CATEGORY: Cell
HEIGHT: 0.3m   WEIGHT: 1.0kg

Solosis can survive in any environment, since its body is enveloped in a special liquid. It communicates with other Solosis by telepathy.

SWOOBAT

TYPE: Psychic-Flying
CATEGORY: Courting
HEIGHT: 0.9m   WEIGHT: 10.5kg

Swoobat uses its nose to emit sound waves. When a courting male gives off ultrasonic waves, it improves the mood of anyone within range.

VICTINI

TYPE: Psychic-Fire
CATEGORY: Victory
HEIGHT: 0.4m   WEIGHT: 4.0kg

Victini is the Pokémon that brings victory, and it's said that the Trainer with Victini always wins. It generates an endless supply of energy to share.

WOOBAT

TYPE: Psychic-Flying
CATEGORY: Bat
HEIGHT: 0.4m   WEIGHT: 2.1kg

Woobat lives in dark caves and forests. When it wants to sleep, the suction of its nostrils helps it cling to a cavern wall.

TRAINER TREASURE BOX

Every Trainer needs a treasure box – it's the perfect place for storing Gym Badges, souvenirs and mementos! Here are Ash's instructions for making your own Unova-themed case. Don't forget to personalize the box so that it features the characters and Pokémon you love the most.

Use the pages of this annual to inspire your drawings. You could also add pictures of Ash, Iris and Cilan or even a self-portrait. Why not draw your name in bubble letters?

YOU WILL NEED:

WHITE PAPER   PENCILS AND FELT-TIP PENS   RULER
SCISSORS   STIFF CARDBOARD BOX WITH A LID (A SHOEBOX WORKS WELL)
GLUE STICK   GLITTER   DECOUPAGE SEALANT OR PVA GLUE   PAINT BRUSH

STEP ONE

Find a pencil then draw lots of pictures of your favourite Pokémon on the sheets of white paper, making each one no more than 10 centimetres tall. You will need to create enough to cover the sides of the box and the lid in overlapping layers. Colour each one in.

STEP TWO

Cut each of the pictures out as neatly as you can. Now use a glue stick to fix the pictures onto your cardboard box. Keep going until the entire box and lid are covered, making sure that there are no gaps between the pictures.

STEP THREE

Pour some decoupage sealant or PVA glue into an old saucer, then sprinkle in a little glitter. Mix the glitter and sealant together, then brush it all over the box and the lid. Leave both pieces to dry.

STEP FOUR

After a few hours, your Trainer treasure box should be ready! Fill it with your favourite trading cards, figurines and keepsakes, then stash it somewhere safe.

BE SCISSOR SAFE!
Ask an adult to help you with the cutting stages.

ZOOM ZONE

Iris has come across all kinds of fascinating Pokémon during her travels through Vertress City. Look through the camera lenses. Can you spy six more species? Try and identify every one.

SMELL AND SEEK

Trubbish aren't the most savoury of Pokémon – the stench from their gassy belches can send a Trainer to sleep! Can you help Garbodor spot its four Trubbish pals? Peer through the crowds and circle each one.

A CHALLENGE FROM ASH

You've followed Ash all over Vertress City, so how much have your learnt about the most go-getting Trainer in the Unova League? This quick quiz will test your knowledge to the limit! Set a timer or stopwatch to five minutes and give it your best shot.

1

WHICH OF THESE POKÉMON IS NOT ONE OF ASH'S?

◇   ◇   ◇

2

WHAT MAKES ASH'S KROOKODILE DIFFERENT TO MOST OTHERS?

5

WHO IS THE PROFESSOR WHO ADVISES ASH IN THE UNOVA REGION?

3

THIS IS ANOTHER OF ASH'S POKÉMON. WHAT IS ITS NAME?

4

WHAT IS THE NAME OF ASH'S HOMETOWN?

6

ONE OF ASH'S POKÉMON IS A POISON-TYPE. WHICH IS IT?

◇   ◇   ◇

7

ASH'S OSHAWOTT CERTAINLY HAS A MIND OF ITS OWN! HOW DOES IT USE ITS SCALCHOP?

8

WHAT WILL ASH'S SCRAGGY EVENTUALLY EVOLVE INTO?

STRONG STRATEGY STEALS THE SHOW!

The Unova League battle excitement continues at a frenzied pace in Vertress City, with Ash advancing to the third round. As his match prepares to get underway, our hero's opponent is none other than his friend and rival Stephan!

Ash watched Stephan's Liepard prowl up and down before him. His friend couldn't have picked a more formidable opponent to kick off the third round!

"I know who I'm using," muttered the Trainer. "Krookodile, I choose you!"

The crowd roared its approval as Krookodile took its place in the arena. Iris, Bianca and Cilan craned forward to look at the Pokémon's snapping jaws and spiny tail.

"Going head to head against a Dark-type with a Dark-type," remarked Cilan. "That's the flavour of a pure Ash strategy!"

"I can't wait to see who's the winner!" chipped in Bianca.

The friends gazed up at the massive Vertress City stadium. It was a packed house. Spectators had arrived in their thousands to see the third round clashes. Ash needed to stay calm and focussed for the challenge ahead.

"You ready Stephan?" shouted Ash.

His rival didn't need any encouragement.

"Yep!" he replied. "So bring it on!"

Up in the commentary box, presenter Freddy the Scoop switched on the mic.

"Hey folks! I'm here to bring you all the play-by-play battle action! Get ready for the Unova League third round!"

The arena went wild with applause.

"First up," continued Freddy, "we've got Ash versus Stephan. Each Trainer may use up to three Pokémon, and you can be sure that this will be one exciting match!"

Now the crowd went silent, waiting in anticipation for someone to make the first move.

"Now Liepard," bellowed Stephan. "Shadow Claw, let's go!"

Ash responded the best way he knew how — with a blistering Dragon Claw attack. This battle was going to be fast and furious from the very start!

"Right off the bat a Shadow Claw and Dragon Claw collision!" exclaimed Freddy the Scoop.
Bang!
The arena shook as Liepard and Krookodile slammed into each other.
"Is it a draw?" called Ash, hopefully.
"No way!" retorted Stephan. "Liepard, Shadow Ball!"
Ash had to think quickly – Stephan wasn't going to budge an inch in his pursuit of the Unova League trophy! The Trainer responded with Krookodile's Stone Edge move, pulling off another draw.
"That's the result of blending Ash and Stephan's strong and direct strategies," commented Cilan.
"Neither one of them is giving an inch," agreed Bianca.
Keen to snatch an advantage, Liepard followed up with a Hyper Beam blast. Its brilliant laser scorched a line through the ground, but Krookodile used Dig to get itself out of harm's way.
"Krookodile successfully dodges Hyper Beam," said Freddy the Scoop. "This could mean an attack from underground!"

Stephan called for Double Team. Krookodile leapt out of its trench, but when it tried to attack it found itself unable to do damage against a crowd of Liepard copies.
"Oh man…" groaned Ash.
Stephan spotted his chance, going straight in with another Shadow Claw. There was no time for Krookodile to dodge – especially when Liepard hammered the attack home with Shadow Ball.
"Hang in there!" urged Ash. He couldn't lose the third round like this!
Sweat poured from Krookodile's brow, but the mighty Pokémon wasn't about to give up the fight quite yet. Slowly and with great determination, it brought itself back up to its full height.
"Way to go!" cheered Ash. "Stone Edge, now!"
Krookodile focussed, then battered its enemy with a tirade of rocks. Now it was Liepard's time to get knocked down!
The seconds ticked by until Stephan's Pokémon finally stood up again.
"Double Team!" repeated Stephan. "One more time!"
Ash's face dropped as Liepard replicated itself all over the arena. There was no way that Krookodile would be able to dodge all of these Pokémon foes. He needed to think up a smart strategy in double quick time!

Ash's mind was racing – Krookodile had to Dig itself out of danger! As the Pokémon buried itself into the ground, Stephan nodded his head.

"Just what I thought," he called triumphantly. "Aim Hyper Beam into that hole!"

Ash cried out in shock as the Liepard duplicates focussed their energies on Krookodile. The submerged Pokémon found itself being blasted from a dozen different angles!

"Krookodile!" begged Ash. "You've got to hang tough. Use Dragon Claw!"

The crowd gasped as Krookodile's triple claws began to glow with raw power. Stephan showed no fear. Instead he sent Liepard to meet its foe face-on.

"Intercept with Shadow Claw!"

The two titans tore towards each other, meeting in a monumental mid-air clash that shook the very foundations of the arena. Both Pokémon were sent reeling to the ground.

"A draw?" wondered Iris again.

"I doubt it," guessed Cilan. "It seems a lot more likely that Krookodile gained some extra momentum as it was falling."

This battle however, wasn't over yet. Krookodile and Liepard eyed each other angrily for an instant, before going back on the attack.

"Shadow Claw, go!" thundered Stephan.

"Dragon Claw, go!" countered Ash.

The Pokémon met again in another awesome smash. The opponents fell to the ground, stunned by the force of the encounter. Had Liepard and Krookodile both met their match?

The crowd waited in stunned silence for something to happen. Ash and Stephan could only watch too, hoping against hope that their Pokémon would be the one to drag itself back into the game.

"Lie-pard, no!"

Stephan's predatory Dark-type rolled onto its side, exhausted by the fray.

"Liepard is unable to battle," confirmed the judge. "Krookodile's the winner!"

Ash couldn't believe his eyes – Krookodile had done it! Beating such a worthy opponent as Liepard was an awesome achievement.

Stephan praised Liepard, then braced himself for the next phase in the battle.

"All right number two!" he shouted. "Go Zebstrika!"

Zebstrika scraped its hoof on the ground impatiently. It was ready for action!

Ash checked out Zebstrika's Pokédex entry before deciding how to respond.

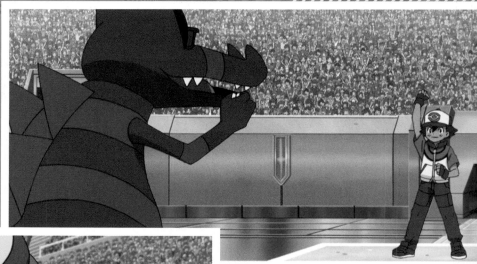

ZEBSTRIKA
THE THUNDERBOLT POKÉMON
Zebstrika moves at lightning-quick speed, producing the sound of thunder at a full gallop.

Ash weighed up his options. Krookodile had taken a lot of damage against Liepard. He decided to let the Dark-type rest up for now. Instead he hurled a different Poké Ball into the arena.

"Palpitoad, I choose you!"

"It's the perfect Pokémon ingredient to create a powerful recipe to battle his opponent with!" praised Cilan.

Bianca seemed confused.

"See, Stephan's Zebstrika's most effective moves are Thunderbolt and Flame Charge, explained the Connoisseur, "but since Palpitoad is a Water- and Ground-type, Electric-type moves won't have any effect and Fire-type moves won't do much at all!"

It appeared that Ash had launched a smart strategy... until the battle began.

"Palpitoad, use Mud Shot!" shouted Ash.

Zebstrika dodged the attack with astonishing speed, before pounding its enemy with a merciless Stomp.

Cilan blinked in surprise.

"Stephan's made certain that Zebstrika knows a variety of moves so it's able to handle Water- and Ground-type opponents, too!"

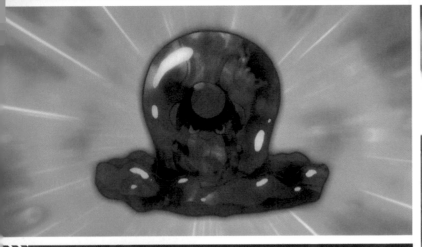

Luckily, Ash also had some new moves up his sleeve. "Palpitoad!" he shouted. "Sludge Wave!"

The spectators watched Palpitoad generate a purple ball of poisonous sludge. The goo pelted Zebstrika between the ears, covering it in toxins. The Pokémon stood motionless, welded to the spot.

"Uh-oh," reported Freddy the Scoop. "Looks like Zebstrika's been poisoned by Sludge Wave."

Any other Trainer would have been crushed, but Stephan launched straight into a Façade counter-attack. The force of the blow sent Palpitoad slamming into the arena wall.

"When a Pokémon with a status condition uses Façade, the move's power gets a huge boost," whispered Cilan.

"I guess Stephan must have been thinking way ahead," agreed Iris.

Cilan was confused. How could Stephan have known that Palpitoad had learned Sludge Wave in the first place? Bianca had a theory – perhaps he had planned ahead in case of a status condition. Stephan's forward thinking had certainly paid off big-style!

Freddy the Scoop waited for Ash to respond, but there was nothing that the Trainer could do.

"Palpitoad has taken a lot of damage," he concluded. "Is this battle over?"

"Let's finish this!" interrupted Stephan. "Wrap this up with Façade!"

Palpitoad began to rouse. Ash sent the Poison-type in with a Supersonic attack that sliced powerfully through the air. The move was super-effective, confusing Zebstrika so much it began bashing its head against the wall!

"No!" wailed Stephan. "You're hurting yourself! Zebstrika, get a grip!"

Now it was Ash's turn to finish the match. Water gushed from Palpitoad's mouth as it pulled off a stunning Hydro Pump. Instead of buckling however, Zebstrika seemed to absorb the bombardment, replying with Giga Impact.

"Palpitoad!!" urged Ash. "Use Mud Shot, go!"

Both Palpitoad and Zebstrika were sent reeling towards the wall. Stephan and Ash waited for the smoke to clear, but it was hopeless – both Pokémon were out of the match!

The judge called time.

"Palipoad versus Zebstrika ends in a draw!"

Ash and Stephan praised their Pokémon, then psyched themselves up for the next challenge. Ash had two Pokémon left to Stephan's one, but Krookodile had already taken a lot of damage.

"All right," announced Stephan, hurling his Poké Ball into the arena. "You're up next! Let's go!"

Ash nodded knowingly as Sawk appeared.

The crowds waited to hear Ash's selection. Within moments, the Bug-Grass-type Leavanny appeared.

Cilan hoped that Ash had made the right choice – could Leavanny really overwhelm an opponent with magnificent rippling muscles like Sawk? The Trainer would have to have a good strategy up his sleeve!

"Leavanny!" called Ash. "String Shot, go!"

Quick as a flash, Leavanny tied Sawk up in its sinewy thread. Unfortunately for Ash, it didn't last long. Sawk bulked up its muscles and broke through the bands.

SAWK
THE KARATE POKÉMON
Sawk's punches get more powerful when it ties its belt. It gets angry when its training is interrupted.

"Use Razor Leaf!" yelled Ash at just the right moment.

Leavanny obeyed instantly, before pulling off a searing Energy Ball. The crowd gasped. The power of Leavanny's counterattack had knocked Sawk to the ground!

"Close Combat!" countered Stephan, keen to take back control.

Ash's Pokémon impressed the crowds with its graceful dodging, before landing an explosive X-Scissor attack.

"Leavanny floats like a Butterfree and stings like a Beedrill!" praised Freddy the Scoop.

Ash chuckled. He had spent a lot of time working with Leavanny to raise its speed – now his training regime was paying off! He knew better than to underestimate his rival quite yet however.

"Use your focus, Sawk!" urged Stephan. "Consecutive Karate Chops!"

A battery of blows came screaming towards Leavanny, but it was ready. In an almost effortless show of skill, it dodged each attack.

"Sawk," pleaded Stephan. "Come on, get up!"

Sawk staggered to its feet, but before the Pokémon could gather its defences Leavanny struck with an X-Scissor.

"Wow!"

Ash was astonished to see Sawk reach up and catch the X-Scissor with both hands! It pushed back at Leavanny, striking it down with its Close Combat move. Leavanny tingled with light. Even though it had taken a lot of damage, the Pokémon appeared more energized than ever!

"What's going on?" asked Iris.

"Swarm, Leavanny's special ability has been activated," explained Cilan. "When a Pokémon with this ability is low on energy, its Bug-type moves increase in power!"

"So cool!" nodded Bianca.

Ash grinned. Now he had to maximize his position! The Trainer sent Leavanny in with another String Shot.

Suddenly the Fighting-type was cocooned in a silken straight jacket. Sawk's muscles were rendered useless — even its trademark Bulk Up move couldn't help it burst out of Leavanny's threads.

"X-Scissor," ordered Ash. "Again and again!"

Leavanny struck its foe, knocking Sawk around the arena. The situation looked dire, but Stephan was quick to spot a way of turning Leavanny's attacks into an opportunity.

"You can use those X-Scissors to your advantage," he insisted, "and cut those threads off!"

Sawk began to turn itself from side to side, hoping to use the glancing blows to slice through the threads. At first it didn't seem to be working – Leavanny got faster and faster as its momentum grew.

"Either those threads will be cut or Sawk won't be able to continue battling," warned Cilan.

"Come on Sawk," hissed Stephan. "Stay focused!"

"Let's finish it up with X-Scissor!" replied Ash, not budging an inch.

Sawk twisted and turned again and again. The crowd roared as the silken bands dropped to the ground.

"The threads have been cut!" confirmed Freddy the Scoop, "but Sawk's taken a lot of damage."

Stephan ignored the commentator, sending his Pokémon straight in with a Karate Chop. The blow was blinding and true, striking Leavanny firmly on its crest. Ash watched in dismay as it fell back onto the dirt.

The judge stepped forward.

"Leavanny is unable to battle! Sawk is the winner!"

Suddenly Sawk raced towards Krookodile. Its muscles rippled as it prepared to strike using Close Combat.

"Counter it with Dragon Claw!" shouted Ash.

Krookodile raised its triple claw, each talon now glowing with raw energy.

Cr-ash!

The Vertress City stadium shook as the titans both attacked with all their might. The Pokémon punched and jabbed at a lightning pace, but when they retreated Krookodile sank to the ground.

Leavanny had battled hard, but this match was over. Now Ash only had one Pokémon left – Krookodile! The Ground-Dark-type dutifully took its place in the arena, but it still seemed fatigued from its clash with Liepard.

Ash's friends waited nervously for the combat to start.

"Poor Krookodile," sighed Iris. "It still doesn't look very good."

Cilan agreed, pointing out that the type match-up also put it at a big disadvantage.

"Dark-type moves aren't very effective against Fighting-types," he explained. "On top of that, Fighting-type moves are super-effective battling Dark-types!"

"Yeah, but Sawk used up a lot of energy in the last battle, right?" remarked Bianca.

The friends looked across at Stephan's Pokémon. Sawk was still panting, but it tightened its belt purposely. Did it have the strength to win through?

"No doubt Sawk's got plenty of energy left!" insisted Stephan. "This battle's ours, Ash!"

Ash laughed. "You'll have to do more than just talk!"

"That's exactly what we're going to do!" replied his rival.

"Is Krookodile running out of steam?" questioned Freddy the Scoop.

Cilan frowned.

"One more move like that one and Krookodile's through!"

Ash clenched his fists, willing his Pokémon to rally.

"Come on, Ash," urged Iris. "Think!"

"All right," decided Stephan, eager to inflict more punishment, "Use Karate Chop!"

Ash took a deep breath.

"Krookodile," he called confidently. "Aerial Ace, let's go!"

"No way?"

Stephan couldn't believe his eyes. Aerial Ace was a Flying-type move that was super-effective against Fighting-types!

Krookodile climbed high in the air, then dive-bombed Sawk with cool, eye-watering precision. Stephan gasped. Sawk had been knocked out in a single blow!

"Sawk's unable to battle," called the judge. "Krookodile's the winner! So the match goes to Ash!"

"I knew you were going to use Sawk in your last battle," grinned Ash, "so I saved up Aerial Ace until the very end!"

Stephan was impressed.

"Pretty smart. Even if I did lose, it was a great battle!"

"Let's give a big round of applause to Ash and Stephan for showing us some serious Unova League battling spirit!" said Freddy the Scoop.

The crowd cheered and screamed their approval from the stands. Iris, Bianca and Cilan leapt to their feet.

"Talk about an awesome battle!" gushed Iris.

"My heart's beating about a million miles an hour!" agreed Bianca.

Cilan gave the contest a Connoisseur's thumbs-up.

"It was a delightfully savoury blend of power versus power and skill versus skill!"

Ash was totally psyched – now he was through to the quarter-finals!

"Way to go!" he cheered. "You were so awesome, Krookodile!"

Stephan was disappointed, but he accepted defeat gracefully. Despite the outcome, Sawk had battled like a champ. He promised the Pokémon a well-deserved rest. In the meantime, the Trainer was keen to find out more about Ash's strategy.

When they got back to the Pokémon Centre, Ash and Stephan couldn't wait to eat. The quarter-finals would be starting the next morning – full battles with six Pokémon per side. Ash's opponent this time would be Cameron.

"I made you a feast!" announced Cilan, as soon as they got to the dining room. Your favourite croquettes with all the trimmings. Fit for a champion!"

"They look great!" grinned Stephan."And Ash, I bet I can eat more than you can!"

Ash was weary, but this was a challenge he couldn't resist!

"So how about having a contest and finding out?"

After dinner, Ash and Pikachu took a run out to the stadium.

"Just think," he muttered. "We're fighting Cameron here tomorrow!"

He looked across the battle arena and spotted a tent in the corner. It had to belong to Cameron and Riolu!

"I was just thinking I can't be late for our battle tomorrow," shrugged the Trainer, climbing out to say hi.

Ash grinned – that was so Cameron! He felt his chest thump as his rival talked about the secret weapon he'd be bringing to the quarter-final.

"Whatever Pokémon you bring I'll be ready for you," promised Ash.

"Yeah?" grinned Cameron. "Not as ready as me!"

The next morning, the whole of Vertress City turned out to watch the fourth round of the Unova League. Ash and Cameron took their places in the battle arena.

"Well... this is it!" said Ash, bracing himself for the challenge ahead.

Cameron hurled his Poké Ball into the air.

"And this is my secret weapon. Let's go!"

Ash gasped in surprise. Cameron's secret weapon was Hydreigon – a brutal Pokémon with six wings!

The quarter-finals have started with a bang! Cameron's secret weapon will take some beating, but rest assured, Ash won't be deterred. Whatever the outcome, our hero is certain to give it everything he's got!

SYMBOL SEEKER

When it comes to seeking out his opponent, Trip never misses a trick! How sharp are your observation skills? Study the four Energy symbols. The exact sequence is only replicated once in the grid below. Can you find it?

ADVANTAGE ASH!

During his time in Unova, Ash has built up an enviable collection of Pokémon. Each one is shown itself to be plucky, trusty and loyal.

Find your boldest pens or pencils, then bring Team Ketchum to life!

3 ON 3

Gear yourself up Pokémon puzzlers, this page offers three knockout tests in one! Give your word power a workout, solve the sequence and then follow the trail. Only top Trainers will be able to ace this 3 on 3.

1. FIND THE NAMES IN THE WORDSEARCH GRID.

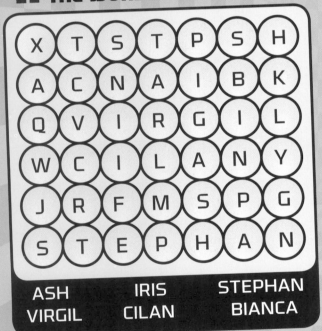

X	T	S	T	P	S	H
A	C	N	A	I	B	K
Q	V	I	R	G	I	L
W	C	I	L	A	N	Y
J	R	F	M	S	P	G
S	T	E	P	H	A	N

ASH   IRIS   STEPHAN
VIRGIL   CILAN   BIANCA

2. WHO IS TRIP GOING TO SEE?

VANILLITE   SERPERIOR   TRANQUILL

3. WHICH POKÉMON SHOULD COME NEXT?

SAWK SEARCH

Sawk can't wait to battle Leavanny but the Grass-type Pokémon has trapped the muscle-bound Pokémon within its sticky silk. Help Sawk find the way back to the battle with Leavanny by drawing a route through the maze of threads.

BEARTIC

TYPE: Ice
CATEGORY: Freezing
HEIGHT: 2.6m   WEIGHT: 260.0kg

Beartic can freeze its breath to create icy fangs and claws for battle. This adept swimmer inhabits northern areas, where it catches prey in the sea.

CRYOGONAL

TYPE: Ice
CATEGORY: Crystallizing
HEIGHT: 1.1m   WEIGHT: 148.0kg

Cryogonal originates inside snow clouds and snags its prey with chains of ice crystals. It turns to steam and vanishes if its body temperature rises.

CUBCHOO

TYPE: Ice
CATEGORY: Chill
HEIGHT: 0.5m   WEIGHT: 8.5kg

Cubchoo sniffs its perpetually runny nose – the mucus is needed for its moves. When Cubchoo is unwell, the mucus becomes watery, decreasing its power.

VANILLISH

TYPE: Ice
CATEGORY: Icy Snow
HEIGHT: 1.1m   WEIGHT: 41.0kg

Vanillish creates hides among ice particles to conceal itself from foes. It dwells in snowy mountains, but migrated to southern areas during an ancient ice age.

VANILLITE

TYPE: Ice
CATEGORY: Fresh Snow
HEIGHT: 0.4m   WEIGHT: 5.7kg

Formed from icicles bathed in morning sunlight, Vanillite's breath is as cold as –58° F. It causes snow to fall around itself by creating snow crystals.

VANILLUXE

TYPE: Ice
CATEGORY: Snowstorm
HEIGHT: 1.3m   WEIGHT: 57.5kg

Vanilluxe creates snow clouds inside its body and attacks foes with fierce blizzards. If both heads get angry at the same time, it buries everything around it.

ARCHEN

TYPE: Rock-Flying
CATEGORY: First Bird
HEIGHT: 0.5m   WEIGHT: 9.5kg

This Pokémon, which was revived from a Fossil, is thought to be the ancestor of all avian Pokémon. Archen hops from branch to branch.

ARCHEOPS

TYPE: Rock-Flying
CATEGORY: First Bird
HEIGHT: 1.4m   WEIGHT: 32.0kg

Archeops uses a running start to take to the air. It is smart enough to cooperate to hunt prey, which it chases by running as fast as a car.

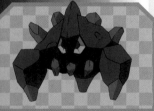

BOLDORE

TYPE: Rock
CATEGORY: Ore
HEIGHT: 0.9m   WEIGHT: 102.0kg

Boldore searches caves for underground water. When it can't contain excess energy, orange crystals form on its body, glowing when its power overflows.

GIGALITH

TYPE: Rock
CATEGORY: Compressed
HEIGHT: 1.7m   WEIGHT: 260.0kg

Gigalith's crystals absorb solar energy, which it amplifies and fires from its mouth. This focused energy powers an attack strong enough to blow apart a mountain.

ROGGENROLA

TYPE: Rock
CATEGORY: Mantle
HEIGHT: 0.4m   WEIGHT: 18.0kg

First discovered a hundred years ago in an earthquake fissure, Roggenrola has a body as hard as steel. Each one has a hexagonal ear and an internal energy core.

TERRAKION

TYPE: Rock-Fighting
CATEGORY: Cavern
HEIGHT: 1.9m   WEIGHT: 260.0kg

It is strong enough to break through a huge castle wall in a single charge. It defended Pokémon forced from their homes by war between humans.

COBALION

TYPE: Steel-Fighting
CATEGORY: Iron Will
HEIGHT: 2.1m   WEIGHT: 250.0kg

Calm and collected, this Pokémon has a body and heart of steel. Cobalion's glare demands instant obedience even from ill-behaved Pokémon.

KLANG

TYPE: Steel
CATEGORY: Gear
HEIGHT: 0.6m   WEIGHT: 51.0kg

To express its feelings, Klang alters its direction of rotation, rotating faster when angry. It can spin its minigears at high speed and fire them at foes.

KLINK

TYPE: Steel
CATEGORY: Gear
HEIGHT: 0.3m   WEIGHT: 21.0kg

Each Klink is composed of two interlocking minigears that rotate to generate its vital energy. Only the right two minigears can successfully mesh together.

KLINGKLANG

TYPE: Steel
CATEGORY: Gear
HEIGHT: 0.6m   WEIGHT: 81.0kg

Klinklang's core is an energy tank. To generate a quick energy charge, the gear with the core spins and Klinklang fires the charged energy from its spikes.

ALOMOMOLA

TYPE: Water
CATEGORY: Caring
HEIGHT: 1.2m   WEIGHT: 31.6kg

Alomomola floats through the open sea surrounded by a special membrane that heals wounds. It embraces injured Pokémon and takes them to shore.

BASCULIN

TYPE: Water
CATEGORY: Hostile
HEIGHT: 1.0m   WEIGHT: 18.0kg

Basculin is hostile — its two forms don't get along and fight each other on sight. Sometimes, however, members of one group will mingle with another.

CARRACOSTA

TYPE: Water-Rock
CATEGORY: Prototurtle
HEIGHT: 1.2m   WEIGHT: 81.0kg

Carracosta can live in water or on land. It can puncture a tanker hull with one slap, and can chew up rocks along with its prey.

DEWOTT

TYPE: Water
CATEGORY: Discipline
HEIGHT: 0.8m   WEIGHT: 24.5kg

Dewott learns its flowing double-Scalchop techniques through rigorous training. The Pokémon always keeps its Scalchops in good condition.

DUCKLETT

TYPE: Water-Flying
CATEGORY: Water Bird
HEIGHT: 0.5m   WEIGHT: 5.5kg

An excellent diver, Ducklett swims around in search of peat moss, its favorite food. If attacked, it splashes water to cover its escape.

FRILLISH

TYPE: Water-Ghost
CATEGORY: Floating
HEIGHT: 1.2m   WEIGHT: 33.0kg

Frillish drags its prey down to its lair after paralysing it with poison. It wraps its veil-like arms around a target, then sinks to the ocean floor.

JELLICENT

TYPE: Water-Ghost
CATEGORY: Floating
HEIGHT: 2.2m   WEIGHT: 135.0kg

This Pokémon propels itself by expelling seawater from its body. Sometimes entire ships and crew vanish after entering Jellicent territory.

OSHAWOTT

TYPE: Water
CATEGORY: Sea Otter
HEIGHT: 0.5m   WEIGHT: 5.9kg

The detachable scalchop on Oshawott's stomach is made from the same material as claws. Oshawott uses the scalchop like a blade to slash at foes.

PALPITOAD

TYPE: Water-Ground
CATEGORY: Vibration
HEIGHT: 0.8m   WEIGHT: 17.0kg

Palpitoad creates water waves or ground tremors by vibrating the bumps on its head. It snares prey with a long, sticky tongue.

PANPOUR

TYPE: Water
CATEGORY: Spray
HEIGHT: 0.6m   WEIGHT: 13.5kg

Panpour doesn't do well in dry environments. To keep itself damp, it stores water in its head tuft and uses its tail as a water-sprayer.

SAMUROTT

TYPE: Water
CATEGORY: Formidable
HEIGHT: 1.5m   WEIGHT: 94.6kg

Samurott's cry intimidates foes, and its glare silences them. The huge blade on its forelegs is part of its armour, taking down an opponent in one hit.

SEISMITOAD

TYPE: Water-Ground
CATEGORY: Vibration
HEIGHT: 1.5m   WEIGHT: 62.0kg

Seismitoad battles using vibrations — it powers up punches by vibrating the bumps on its fists. The bumps on its head shoot a paralysing liquid.

SIMIPOUR

TYPE: Water
CATEGORY: Geyser
HEIGHT: 1.0m   WEIGHT: 29.0kg

Simipour stores water in its head tufts. When the level is low, it siphons up more with its tail. This tail can also shoot out water.

SWANNA

TYPE: Water-Flying
CATEGORY: White Bird
HEIGHT: 1.3m   WEIGHT: 24.2kg

It can whip its neck around to deliver powerful attacks with its bill. At dusk, a Swanna flock dances with the flock's leader in the middle.

TIRTOUGA

TYPE: Water-Rock
CATEGORY: Prototurtle
HEIGHT: 0.7m   WEIGHT: 16.5kg

Restored from a Fossil, Tirtouga lived in the oceans about 100 million years ago and can dive to depths of a kilometre or more.

TYMPOLE

TYPE: Water
CATEGORY: Tadpole
HEIGHT: 0.5m   WEIGHT: 4.5kg

Tympole generates sounds beyond human hearing range by vibrating its cheeks. To warn others of danger, it makes a high-pitched noise.

Cameron's secret weapon is unexpected, to say the least! Ash needs to learn all he can about Hydreigon, but his Pokédex is malfunctioning! Can you help Ash by drawing and filling in the info from your Pokédex on the left into Ash's on the right?

Hydreigon. The Brutal Pokémon and the evolved form of Zweilous. Hydreigon believes anything that moves is its opponent, viciously attacking with its three heads.

BRING HYDREIGON TO LIFE BY ADDING SOME COLOUR!

ANSWERS

PAGE 6. GET TO KNOW... ASH
1.B, 2.B, 3.A

PAGE 7. GET TO KNOW... PIKACHU
1.A, 2.C, 3.C

PAGE 8. GET TO KNOW... IRIS
1.B, 2.B, 3.A

PAGE 9. GET TO KNOW... CILAN
1.C, 2.C, 3.B

PAGE 10. GET TO KNOW... BIANCA
1.A, 2.C, 3.B

PAGE 11. GET TO KNOW... TRIP
1.B, 2.C, 3.A

PAGE 12. GET TO KNOW... OFFICER JENNY
1.A, 2.C

PAGE 12. GET TO KNOW... NURSE JOY
1.C, 2.B

PAGE 13. GET TO KNOW... PROF. JUNIPER
1.C, 2.B

PAGE 13. GET TO KNOW... TEAM ROCKET
1.B, 2.A

PAGE 28. SERPERIOR SPOT
Pictures A and I

PAGE 29. TRAINING TEST
Ash is going to have a training battle with <u>CAMERON</u>

PAGE 32. SHATTERED SCREEN
1.E, 2.C, 3.B, 4.A, 5.D

PAGE 33. FLAME GAME
<u>DOWN:</u> 1. Stomach, 2. Pignite, 3. Darumaka, 4. Red, 5. Cold
<u>ACROSS:</u> 1. Simsear, 2. Angry, 3. Heatmor, 4. Beard

PAGE 34. PERFECT MATCH
A. Oshawott   B. Escavalier   C. Samurott

PAGE 35. A ROUTE FOR RIOLU

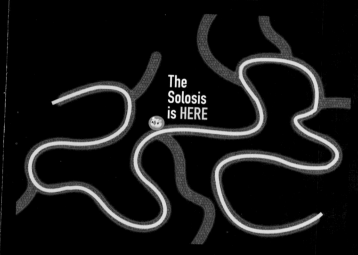

The Solosis is HERE

PAGE 56. SMELL AND SEEK

PAGE 68. SYMBOL SEEKER

PAGE 70. 3 ON 3

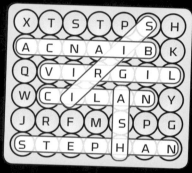

VANILLITE   SERPERIOR   TRANQUILL

PAGE 71. SAWK SEARCH

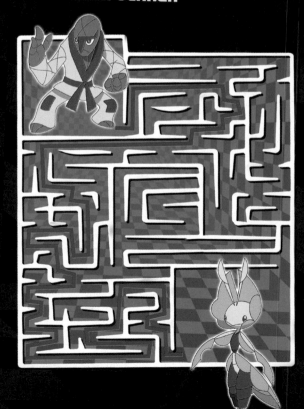

Pokémon Annual 2014

Visit **Pedigreebooks.com** to find out more on this year's **Pokémon Annual,** scan with your mobile device to learn more.

Visit www.pedigreebooks.com

Pedigree Books, Beech Hill House, Walnut Gardens, Exeter EX4 4DH